The

Anxiety

WORKBOOK

THE ANXIETY WORKBOOK

Copyright © Summersdale Publishers Ltd, 2022

Inspired by *No More Worries!* by Poppy O'Neill (published 2021). Text by Caroline Roope.

All rights reserved.

No part of this book may be reproduced by any means, nor transmitted, nor translated into a machine language, without the written permission of the publishers.

Condition of Sale
This book is sold subject to the condition that it shall not, by way of trade or otherwise, be lent, resold, hired out or otherwise circulated in any form of binding or cover other than that in which it is published and without a similar condition including this condition being imposed on the subsequent purchaser.

An Hachette UK Company
www.hachette.co.uk

Vie Books, an imprint of Summersdale Publishers Ltd
Part of Octopus Publishing Group Limited
Carmelite House
50 Victoria Embankment
LONDON
EC4Y 0DZ
UK

www.summersdale.com

Printed and bound in China

ISBN: 978-1-80007-397-5

Substantial discounts on bulk quantities of Summersdale books are available to corporations, professional associations and other organizations. For details contact general enquiries: telephone: +44 (0) 1243 771107 or email: enquiries@summersdale.com.

The *Anxiety* WORKBOOK

Practical Tips and Guided Exercises to Help You Overcome Anxiety

Anna Barnes

CONTENTS

DISCLAIMER

This book is not intended as a substitute for the medical advice of a doctor or physician. If you are experiencing problems with your health, it is always best to follow the advice of a medical professional.

INTRODUCTION

Welcome to *The Anxiety Workbook*, a guide to understanding and dealing with anxiety, so you can work towards a worry-free life. The first step on a self-help journey can be the hardest, but it's also the most positive. Kudos to you for being proactive and picking up this book.

It's natural for us to feel a little edgy from time to time; after all, life has a knack of throwing stumbling blocks in our way, usually when we least expect it. Work pressures, looking after family, maintaining friendships, and organizing our "life-admin" can feel like a huge juggling act – no wonder when something tips us off balance, we struggle to keep a level head and control our emotions.

It's normal in times of short-term stress to feel anxious; let's not forget that a big part of "adulting" involves overcoming challenges every now and again. But when temporary panic turns into long-term anxiety, every day can feel overwhelming.

Using a mix of ideas, activities and proven techniques used by therapists – such as cognitive behavioural therapy (CBT) and mindfulness – this book will support you in re-shaping your thoughts and emotions, so that you're equipped with an anxiety toolkit to use when life gets challenging.

Anxiety disorders are common across the globe. They can affect anyone, in all walks of life, irrespective of age, gender, race or situation. According to the World Health Organization, 3.6 per cent – or about 286 million individuals worldwide – have an anxiety disorder.

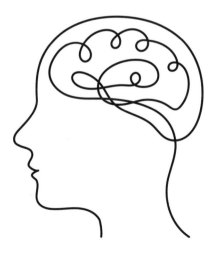

WHAT THIS BOOK
WILL DO FOR YOU

This book will help you gain a better understanding of how your mind and emotions work, and how anxiety affects your whole body. You'll learn how to reset your thoughts so that you can use your mental energy to stay positive and in control, rather than waste your energy on worry.

Life is unpredictable, and we can't always control what happens to us, but we can decide how we choose to cope with it. The more we can learn about ourselves, the greater confidence we'll have in managing our feelings when anxiety threatens to overwhelm us. If you want to turn your anxiety into a source of strength and let go of fear, then you've come to the right place.

You already have all the tools and potential inside of you to help anxiety loosen its grip; you just need a little nudge in the right direction and some self-belief. So read on and remember: anxiety is the thief of joy but you're strong enough to get the better of it – you can do this!

HOW TO USE THIS BOOK

This book is for you if...

- You often feel worried, on edge and irritable.
- You have troubling thoughts or a sense of dread.
- You are struggling to sleep.
- You feel physically ill because of anxiety.
- You feel anxious about aspects of your body, identity or personality.

- You keep quiet about your desires, needs and opinions.
- You get worried about or avoid social situations.
- You struggle to express how you are really feeling or voice your needs.

If that sounds like you sometimes, or even all the time, this book is here to help – but only you have the power to change your outlook for the better.

Inside these pages you'll find advice on how to keep calm and cope with anxiety. You'll start to understand how your feelings, thoughts and behaviours are connected and affect each other as well as how anxiety makes your body feel and how best to react to those physical sensations. You'll also learn strategies to help you face your fears, challenge unhelpful thoughts and re-tune your emotions.

Some of the ideas will be useful and others not so much – you'll be best able to judge what your own needs are. It's a little like going to the gym – but to strengthen your mind instead. The most important thing though, is to take it at a pace that's comfortable and feels right for you.

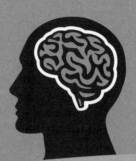

Part 1:

Anxiety and You

WHAT IS ANXIETY?

Anxiety is the body's natural response to feeling under threat. Although it originates in our brain, it's a whole-body experience, affecting our thoughts, feelings, emotions and our physical state too.

When our brains sense danger, a chain of rapidly occurring reactions happen in our body. It's like the brain is shouting "mobilize" and the rest of the body springs into action, ready to deal with the threatening circumstance. This brain chemistry has been keeping us all safe since prehistoric times. In a way, anxiety is the reason humans still exist. Without a sense of danger, life becomes precarious, to say the least!

The trouble is our brains still think we live in prehistoric times, so if we trigger our emotions with a difficult but non-life-threatening situation, it sends out anxiety signals.

Situations such as starting a new job or delivering a presentation are guaranteed to put the calmest of us in a flap. We all know the signs – we breathe a bit faster, our palms feel sweaty, and we can feel our heart beating quicker. We might even feel a bit sick. These are all physical signs of the brain's anxiety response. The good news is, these are all perfectly natural and mercifully short-lived bodily responses to stress that pass when the situation is over. However, when these responses intensify or persist to the point where they are overwhelming, they can start to have a detrimental effect on all areas of our life.

WHAT DOES ANXIETY FEEL LIKE?

Anxiety can show itself in lots of different ways, and one person's experience is often quite different to another's. Some of the most common signs include:

Low sex drive

Loss of appetite

Nausea and/or stomach ache

Pins and needles

Negative thoughts

Excessive worrying

Feeling agitated, irritable and/or snappy

Shallow or fast breathing

Thumping or irregular heartbeat

Headache and muscle tension

Feeling dissociated from the world around you

Hot flushes and/or sweating

Dizziness and lightheadedness

Needing to go to the toilet

Feeling too hot or too cold

An overwhelming sense of doom or dread

Dry mouth and/or feeling thirsty

It can also make us behave differently too. Here are some of the most common ways it can affect our behaviour:

- Craving lots of reassurance from other people or worrying that people are angry or upset with you
- Deliberating over past experiences, or overthinking a situation
- Wanting to shut yourself away from the world
- Lashing out and being aggressive
- Crying or feeling teary several times a day
- Not wanting to get out of bed
- No interest in, or lack of self-care
- Struggling to maintain the demands of a job or home life
- Difficulty in forming or keeping relationships
- Lack of enthusiasm for trying new things
- Nervous behaviours, such as nail biting, lip chewing, scratching your skin or pulling out your hair
- Fidgeting and restlessness
- Difficulty concentrating
- Blaming others for the situation or your behaviour
- Grinding your teeth or clenching your jaw
- Difficulty speaking and/or stumbling over words
- Struggling to articulate yourself
- Shyness
- Struggling to keep eye contact
- Wanting to run away or hide
- Nervous coughing

WHAT DOES ANXIETY FEEL AND LOOK LIKE FOR YOU?

Think of a time recently when you felt anxious, worried or afraid. What did that feel like in your body? How did you react? Write it down below – you can use the examples on the previous page and add your own.

Thinking about and writing down how anxiety feels for you will help you to spot it in future. When you can recognize anxiety, it becomes easier to deal with.

WHY DO WE WORRY?

Good question! If we no longer need to worry about keeping ourselves alive on a minute-by-minute basis, why are we so beset with anxious thoughts?

The problem is, we're bombarded with information about what is going wrong in the world. Not only that, but we're also reminded of all the things that *could* go wrong. As humans we're hardwired to assess threat levels and think about the best way to deal with them, which means we worry about everything from illness, to crime, to money, to global politics – the list is endless. Throw in our own complicated personal lives and that twenty-first-century obsession with comparing ourselves to others and let's just say, a worry-free life it does not make.

Our brains are truly unique. By allowing us to *think*, they have gifted us some of the most remarkable achievements in history, such as inventing the wheel and landing on the moon. Our minds are a gift – but they can also be a curse. Thinking enables us to engage with the world around us in the present. It also helps us to visualize the past and future, and react as though those events are happening *right now*. So, we worry about hypothetical scenarios, as well as worrying about past mistakes and bad situations. The mind's potential to imagine is limitless but the result of this is that it also has a limitless capacity to worry. And when worry starts to make life difficult, then we need to do something about it.

MY ANXIETY

What makes you feel anxious? Perhaps it's a thought that keeps you awake at night or a situation you go out of your way to avoid. It could be a specific life event or several things that worry you every day. Writing it all down is a bit like downloading files to an external hard drive – it frees up space in your head! Write as many of your anxiety triggers as you can think of here:

Example trigger: I have intense anxiety about meeting new people. In this situation I worry I will show my anxiety by stumbling over my words.

The next step is to think about which symptoms bother you the most or make life hardest for you. They could be physical symptoms, such as trembling or a racing heart, or symptoms that affect how you feel, such as your mind going blank or being unable to cope. Jot them down here:

Example symptoms: Meeting new people makes me feel short of breath and gives me a shaky voice. This makes me feel self-conscious and embarrassed.

Finally, take a moment to reflect on what your ideal outcome would be if anxiety were removed from each situation. Having a goal to work towards is important because it allows you to see whether you are making progress. Note it down here:

Example outcome: To be able to enjoy meeting new people and improve my confidence so that I am not worrying that they will judge me.

WHEN ANXIETY TAKES HOLD

Anxiety has the potential to weave its way into our everyday lives. It might make it difficult for you to go to work or form new relationships. It can even make you feel like a prisoner in your own home.

When anxiety takes hold and becomes an even greater problem is when there appears to be no trigger, and it starts to feel like you're existing in a constant state of worry and fear without really knowing why. This is because the brain learns to continuously release stress hormones, leaving your brain flooded with negative thoughts and you feeling constantly overwhelmed. You may feel like you're unable to enjoy even the simplest things and you're just "getting by" from day to day.

In short, you've stopped *living* – you're just surviving.

If this sounds like you, contact your doctor or healthcare provider for further guidance and support.

PANIC ATTACKS

Sometimes an episode of anxiety can come on suddenly and cause an intense reaction, overwhelming you to the point where you feel completely out of control. This is called a panic attack. Most panic attacks last between 5 minutes and half an hour. If you're having a panic attack you might experience:

- **Bodily shaking and tremors**
- **Dizziness**
- **Laboured breathing or breathlessness**
- **A sudden rise in body temperature**
- **Nausea**
- **Disorientation**
- **Sweating and/or feeling clammy**

If you think you're having a panic attack, here are some things you can do to help you cope until it passes:

- **Ask for help from someone you trust – they could sit with you, hug you or hold your hand.**
- **Close your eyes.**
- **Remember that the panic attack will end soon and that it can't hurt you.**
- **Think about your breathing – count to four as you breathe in, then out for four and repeat.**
- **Once the panic attack has passed, be very gentle with yourself. You might feel tired or thirsty, or you might want to move around or get some fresh air. Listen to your body and go slowly.**

Although panic attacks feel really distressing, they can't hurt you. It is simply the feeling of your brain and nervous system setting off an emergency alarm in your body, causing you to feel that "fight, flight or freeze" sense of danger.

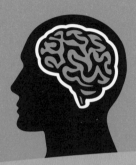

Part 2:

Dealing with Anxiety

Now you've got to know your anxiety a little better and you're beginning to understand how unhelpful it is in your life, it's time to gently start to show it the door. Don't forget, anxiety is perfectly normal some of the time - it's when it starts to affect your day-to-day life that it becomes a problem.

If you feel like you've become trapped in a negative cycle and your anxiety has become a burden, it makes sense to learn some strategies to help yourself get back to living your best life. It isn't a process that happens overnight but take comfort from the fact that you've taken that all-important first step and that better days are on the horizon.

In this chapter we'll look at the best way to attune ourselves to how we think and feel, particularly when we're in the grip of anxiety, and how best to tackle unhelpful thoughts and behaviours.

HOW TO DEAL WITH ANXIETY

So now you know a bit more about what anxiety is and how to recognize it, what can you do about it? Cognitive Behavioural Therapy (CBT) is useful for targeting the three key parts of the anxiety response: how we think, how we feel and what we do.

Thinking: Helps us to question situations that make us anxious and consider how we perceive danger.

Feeling: Helps us to gain a better understanding of our anxiety symptoms and how to manage them.

Doing: Helps us to change our actions by confronting the things we try to avoid.

The aim is to move away from a negative cycle:

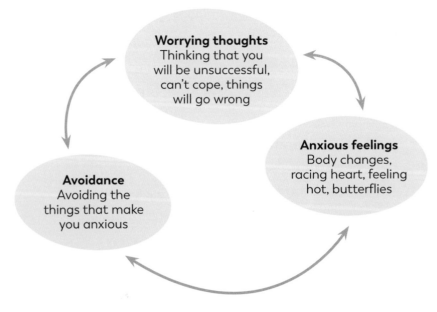

Worrying thoughts
Thinking that you will be unsuccessful, can't cope, things will go wrong

Anxious feelings
Body changes, racing heart, feeling hot, butterflies

Avoidance
Avoiding the things that make you anxious

To a more positive, balanced cycle:

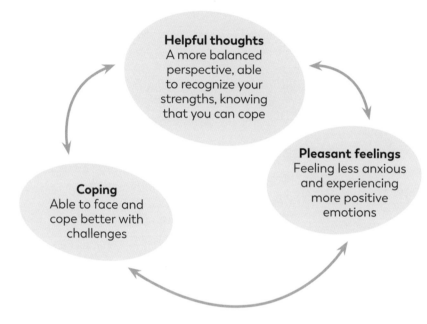

Helpful thoughts
A more balanced perspective, able to recognize your strengths, knowing that you can cope

Pleasant feelings
Feeling less anxious and experiencing more positive emotions

Coping
Able to face and cope better with challenges

Ultimately, no one is anxiety-free – even those super-Zen, chilled-out folks that look like they're drifting through life on a cloud of happiness and have everything down pat (we all know one!). The goal is to learn to cope with anxiety, rather than get rid of it completely. Don't forget, it can be helpful in *some* situations – it can motivate us, give us a push in the right direction, help us achieve remarkable things and, most importantly, protect us from danger. We just don't want it bothering us all the time!

WRITE IT OUT

What's on your mind? In the previous section you wrote about all the things that cause you anxiety. Now it's time to focus on the one thing that's bugging you at this very moment.

There's plenty of room, so keep writing all your thoughts about it here. You can continue, using another piece of paper if you run out of space. If you get stuck you can always use the prompts to help you get started.

I keep thinking about the time...

I'm afraid that...

I'm feeling under pressure to...

I'm nervous about...

I wish I didn't have to...

I worry that...

Writing down your worries is a great way to start dealing with them, and it frees up your headspace for something else.

CALM BRAIN VS ANXIOUS BRAIN

What's it like in your brain when you feel calm? What kinds of things do you think about? For example, it might feel like your mind is as clear as a cloudless sky, or maybe you know that visualizing waves lapping gently on a sandy shore takes you to a good place. There is no right or wrong answer, so don't hold back!

Write down some ideas around your calm brain here; there are some prompts if you need them:

It feels like...

...makes me calm.

When my mind is clear, I feel...

To feel relaxed, I think about....

What's it like in your mind when you're feeling anxious? Perhaps it's taken up with just one thought or image, or maybe there are lots? Does it seem like it's filled with fog? Or do your thoughts tumble around your head as though it's a washing machine? Use words to describe your anxious brain here; there are some prompts to get you started:

When I'm anxious, my mind feels...

Stress makes me think...

Anxiety makes my head feel...

When anxiety becomes overwhelming, it can be difficult to think about anything else. The good news is the exercises on the following pages will help you to develop a toolbox of anxiety-challenging resources you can use to control your thoughts when things get too much. You just need to learn how and when to deploy them!

LISTEN TO YOUR BODY AND MIND

When you feel anxious, that sensation comes from the part of your brain that controls emotions: the amygdala. If your brain senses danger (even if it's not a dangerous situation, just something you're worried about, like a job interview), the amygdala sends feelings of anxiety around your body.

When you start to feel anxiety building, don't try to stop the feeling or pretend it's not there. Instead, take a deep breath and talk yourself through the sensation, a bit like this:

- **I'm feeling anxiety.**
- **I'm safe: feelings can't hurt me.**
- **What is the anxiety trying to tell me?**
- **It's telling me that the interviewer won't like me, I won't get the job and I might never progress in my career.**
- **That might happen: I don't know the future. If it happens, I'll cope. I can't control other people's emotions or how they feel about me.**
- **I can describe the feeling in my body – I feel hot, and my heart is beating fast.**
- **I am safe to feel this and to think these thoughts. This will pass.**

It's also important to listen to your body – what's it really trying to tell you? Our bodies speak to us all day, reminding us what they need to keep us healthy, comfortable and energized; be that food, sleep or exercise. The problem is, we often ignore them – and before we know it, we feel flat, exhausted and a bit bleurgh.

Reconnecting with your body and honouring its needs will also help you to overcome some of the physical symptoms of anxiety.

The easiest way to do this is to use your breath and sense of touch in combination. Try the following:

- **Put your palm over your heart and feel its beat. Feel how your chest rises and falls with each breath. Now close your eyes and take a deep breath, feeling it fill your lungs. Hold it a moment, then exhale slowly.**
- **Continue to breathe deeply in this way, bringing your focus to the sound of your inhale and exhale.**
- **Now, tune into your body and see if you can hear what it's telling you.**

Is it tense? Tired? Restless? Or perhaps it's telling you it's simply hungry or thirsty? See if you can meet that need.

- **If your body is feeling tense, try inhaling deeply and pulling your shoulders all the way up to your ears, then exhaling with a "whoosh". Repeat until you feel calmer.**
- **If you're restless, take a break and walk out your nervous energy.**
- **If your muscles feel stiff, take 5 minutes to stretch them out.**
- **If you're tired, take a power nap. Even 15 minutes can sometimes be enough to give us a boost.**

MINDFUL BREATHING

Mindfulness means paying attention to the present moment. It's a concept that originated in Buddhist philosophy and it's been proven to reduce anxiety, improve concentration and boost self-esteem. You can do almost anything mindfully – eating, working, stroking a pet... All you need to do is focus all your attention on the activity. So, if you're cuddling your dog mindfully, you notice the smell and texture of its fur, the warmth of its body and the emotions you feel. When you do this, your mind doesn't have time to focus on anxious thoughts.

Mindful breathing is a great skill to learn because it's always available to you, wherever you are and whatever you're doing. Here's how:

Take a deep breath in through your nose. Feel the air flowing through your nostrils. Notice your chest and belly expand. Breathe out and feel your body relax, noticing how the air feels as it flows out of your nostrils – is it warmer or cooler than the in-breath? Breathe in again and keep going like this for three breaths, or however long you need.

ALTERNATE NOSTRIL BREATHING

This is another powerful breathing technique that you can use to calm your nervous system in a hurry. It might seem a little strange at first but once you've tried it a few times you'll see what a difference it makes.

Place your fingers against the sides of your nose and use them to control your breath so that you are forced to concentrate on your breathing. This takes your attention away from anxious thoughts, while the increased oxygen delivered to your bloodstream from deep breathing calms your body.

Here's how to do it:

- **First, use one finger to squish down your right nostril.**

- **Take a deep breath in through your left nostril.**

- **Hold your breath while you release your right nostril, swap hands and squish down your left nostril.**

- **Breathe out through your right nostril.**

- **Now do it again, but this time the other way round.**

- **Keep going for five breaths, or until you're ready to stop.**

FIND YOUR RHYTHM

Moving your body helps difficult emotions to move through you. Even taking a stroll around the office or around your garden can help to release endorphins, the hormones that helps us to manage stress. Being active also gives our brains a new focus, diverting our attention away from any anxious thoughts.

It doesn't really matter what type of activity you choose, but studies have found that rhythmic movement is best for calming the nervous system and reducing anxiety.

Dancing

Letting your body move in time to music releases feel-good brain chemicals, as well as getting rid of anxious energy. Singing along at top volume doubles the benefits, because it makes your chest and throat vibrate, soothing your nervous system.

Yoga

Stretching into yoga poses releases tension in your body and helps to improve your ability to tolerate uncomfortable sensations – making it easier for you to cope with anxiety. Yoga also helps you relax, slows your breathing and releases endorphins in your brain. Check online for some simple yoga poses to try.

Walking

Walking off anxiety really works. The rhythm of your footsteps calms your amygdala and nervous system because rhythmic movement signals to this part of your brain that you are safe.

Moving intuitively

This simply means listening to your body; seeing how it wants to move and what it needs. You might find yourself swaying, stretching or even making noises. This one's best to try when you're alone, so you don't worry about what anyone else thinks!

HOW BIG IS MY PROBLEM?

Anxiety can be paralyzing. When you're caught up in anxious thoughts, problems can feel bigger than they truly are. Take a moment to bring your thoughts back down to earth, by thinking logically about how big your problem is.

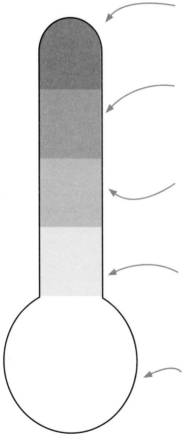

Emergency: fire, serious injury, danger or threat to life
Solution: get help, call the emergency services

Big problem: serious illness, bereavement, relationship breakdown, financial problems, loss of job
Solution: Seek support from family, friends or external agencies

Medium problem: feeling ill, disagreement with friends or family, being slightly injured
Solution: self-care, try again to talk through your problems, ask for help from family and friends

Minor problem: something is broken or lost, someone was rude, paying a bill a bit late
Solution: ask for help, walk away, take steps to fix the situation

Tiny or no problem: being late, making a mistake, burning dinner, forgetting something of minor importance
Solution: it's annoying and feels uncomfortable, but it's manageable; you can cope and then move on!

Even with a tiny problem, you can ask for help. It's OK if your feelings are bigger than the issue. Using a scale like this will help you to work out if there are any steps you can take to solve the problem and lessen your anxiety.

ANXIETY DIARY

Understanding your relationship with anxiety will help you to bring it under control. It's a good idea to keep an anxiety diary so you can make a note of what makes you feel high anxiety, how it feels for you and, crucially, what helps to calm you in these moments.

Keep a record of every time you feel anxious and see if you can learn something from each one.

Date/Time:

What caused the anxious feeling?

What did it feel like?

What thoughts did you have?

Did you try any strategies?

What helped?

What didn't help?

Date/Time:

What caused the anxious feeling?

What did it feel like?

What thoughts did you have?

Did you try any strategies?

What helped?

What didn't help?

Date/Time:

What caused the anxious feeling?

What did it feel like?

What thoughts did you have?

Did you try any strategies?

What helped?

What didn't help?

REVIEW, REFLECT, REACT

After completing the diary, find some quiet time to review it. How did you get on? See if you can find a pattern to your anxiety which will help you manage it.

Is there a particular day or time when you feel anxious? Write it here:

Are there common situations which make you anxious? Write them here:

Are there any common thoughts when you become anxious? Write them here:

Are there any anxiety strategies you use frequently that help? Write how it feels here:

RECOGNIZING THE SIGNS

As we've already discussed, our bodies also alert us to stress via anxiety signals such as a racing heart and a dry mouth. Remember, these sensations are normal; it's just your body responding to what it thinks is danger. It does not mean something is physically wrong with you. If you can recognize what these signals are, it will help you to get the better of your anxiety before it overwhelms you.

   Circle the signs you notice and double-circle the ones that affect you the most. Add in any other signs.

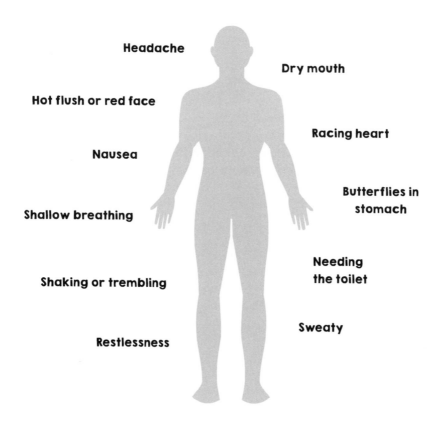

Headache

Dry mouth

Hot flush or red face

Racing heart

Nausea

Butterflies in stomach

Shallow breathing

Needing the toilet

Shaking or trembling

Sweaty

Restlessness

THINGS YOU CAN CONTROL AND THINGS YOU CAN'T

When you're feeling anxious, it's easy to forget what is within your control and what isn't. When something is outside of your control, no amount of anxiety will change it. Not only that, when we become anxious, we often feel very out of control, which makes the situation seem worse than it usually is.

There are many things we cannot control, such as the people around us, what others think of us or what they're feeling, and (unfortunately) the weather! Nonetheless, there are many things we *can* still control. We can control how we choose to respond to a situation and what steps we can take to help ourselves feel less anxious. For instance, if you are anxious about a professional exam, you may not be able to control that you must sit it to progress in your career. You can, however, choose what strategy to use to combat your anxious thoughts, such as breathing exercises, talking through your anxiety with a friend, or practising mindfulness.

When something is within your control, you have the power to act and change it for the better. Use the image on the next page as a visual reminder of all the things that *are* in your control next time you're feeling anxious.

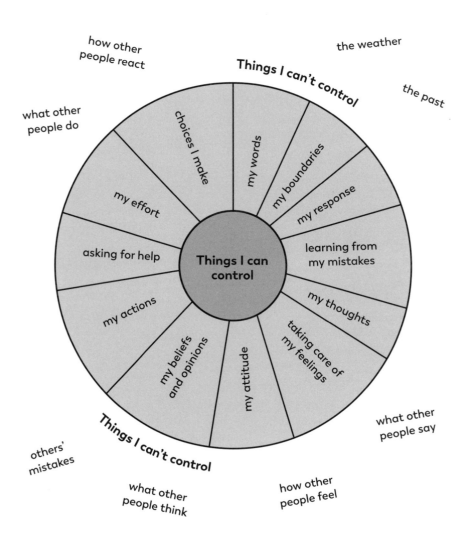

how other
people react

the weather

Things I can't control

the past

what other
people do

choices I make

my words

my boundaries

my effort

my response

asking for help

**Things I can
control**

learning from
my mistakes

my actions

my thoughts

my beliefs
and opinions

my attitude

taking care of
my feelings

Things I can't control

what other
people say

others'
mistakes

what other
people think

how other
people feel

CHANGE YOUR THOUGHTS

It's normal to think negative or critical thoughts from time to time. But anxiety can cause you to think like this *all the time*. The knock-on effect is that it becomes hard to recognize your successes or when you *do* cope because you've become trapped in a cycle of negative and unhelpful thoughts.

We've already learned that thoughts influence feelings and feelings influence actions. It's called the Cognitive Triangle, and it looks like this:

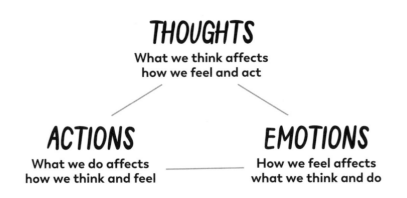

THOUGHTS
**What we think affects
how we feel and act**

ACTIONS
**What we do affects
how we think and feel**

EMOTIONS
**How we feel affects
what we think and do**

So, it makes sense that if you think different thoughts, you'll be able to take more control over your feelings and be able to choose different actions. Changing your thoughts begins with the knowledge that they are not facts: they're stories that we can choose to believe or not... And many of them have massive plot holes.

We can call these plot holes "thinking errors" – let's look at the most common types:

- **Focus on the negatives: that's all I can see – even when something nice happens, I always find a way to feel bad about it.**

- **All-or-nothing thinking: if something isn't perfect, I've failed completely.**

- **Catastrophizing: if a small, bad thing happens, it'll ruin everything.**

- **Mind-reading: I know what other people are thinking about me.**

- **Fortune-telling: I know something will go wrong.**

- **Feelings are facts: I feel like a failure, so I'll fail.**

- **Putting yourself down: I'm useless – I can't do anything.**

- **Perfectionism: I should be perfect at everything. I should never make a mistake or need help.**

- **Blaming: it's all my/their fault!**

Do any of these thinking errors sound familiar? Perhaps you think like this sometimes, or a lot of the time. Can you work out what's wrong with each one? Some of them are just unfair, while others involve predicting the future.

When you're stuck thinking like this, it can feel very real. The best thing to do is talk it all through with a trusted friend or relative. Quite often, this helps to understand where the thoughts could be untrue. In the next chapter, we'll look in detail at how to change your thinking habits so you can use your mind to help calm your anxiety.

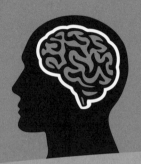

Part 3:
How to Take Control

In the last chapter we identified what your anxiety looks and feels like for you. We also learned that anxiety is a perfectly normal reaction to day-to-day uncertainties such as, "Will I get to work on time?" or "Am I going to be able to pay a bill?" For many of us these thoughts are fleeting and have little impact on our daily lives. For those of us who tend to ruminate and let anxiety control how we think and feel, it's time to shift our mindset and learn how to take that control back again.

LEARNING TO CONTROL YOUR ANXIETY

If we can learn to recognize when our anxiety is about to take hold and remind ourselves that it's just our thoughts – and nothing scarier than that – we have a better chance of keeping it in check. Because we hear our own negativity so often, we start to believe it and don't stop to see whether that niggling, unhelpful voice in our minds is right or not.

One of the first steps in controlling our anxiety is to train ourselves to question our thinking by drawing on past experiences that have had a positive outcome. The more you can remind yourself of the times you've been strong, capable and *have* coped, the more you'll be able to loosen anxiety's grip and talk yourself into a calmer mindset.

Whenever you can feel your anxiety increasing, try using the Catch It, Check It, Challenge It, Change It technique. It works like this:

1   **Catch the unhelpful thought.**
    e.g. "I can't do this: I'm rubbish at my job and should be sacked."

2   **Check the thought: is it justified? Or are you exaggerating? What evidence is there to support that thought?**
    e.g. "Last time I had to perform this task, a colleague told me I was doing it all wrong, but I did manage to finish it."

3   Challenge the thought: what evidence is there that goes against this negative thought? Is there a positive thought you can use to challenge it?
e.g. "My boss said the report I handed in last month was excellent and he's going to share it with the CEO."

4   Change it: is there a more balanced way of thinking about this?
e.g. "I might find it difficult but I coped last time and got really great feedback."

Think of an unhelpful thought you're experiencing now and use it for the activity below. Or you could look back at your anxiety diary and use one from there. Perhaps you're worried you're going to get laughed at when you give a speech next week, or maybe you're worried that people won't like you at your new job. Whatever the thought is that's bothering you, doing this will help you learn to accept your anxiety and be able to put things into perspective.

CATCH IT: What unhelpful thoughts are you having?

CHECK IT: Could you be exaggerating how bad
things are? Can you justify the thought?

CHALLENGE IT: What evidence is there to support the negative thought? Can you think of a positive thought to challenge it?

CHANGE IT: Remembering how you've answered the above, is there a more balanced way of thinking about things?

CALMING YOUR NERVOUS SYSTEM

Remember the different types of anxiety-reducing movement we looked at on page 38? They are all effective ways of calming the nervous system but now it's time to have a think about what works for *your* nervous system. Everyone is unique and one person's calming movement might feel quite stressful for somebody else.

Below are some other activities that can be soothing for the nervous system. Perhaps you'll recognize one or two that you've always found strangely relaxing but you've never realized why before...

- **Singing**
- **Stretching**
- **Swaying**
- **Humming**
- **Household chores**
- **Splashing your face with cold water**
- **Taking a cold shower**
- **Reading aloud**
- **Laughing**

- **Hugging**
- **Stroking and cuddling a pet**
- **Using a weighted blanket**
- **Drumming**
- **Massage**
- **Breathing exercises**
- **Listening to white noise or calming sounds such as waves or forest sounds**

Have a think about what works to calm your nervous system or try some of these ideas. Most importantly, keep an open mind – it may be the thing you least expect!

AFFIRMATIONS

An affirmation is a short, positive sentence designed to help you feel better, calmer, more confident and compassionate towards yourself. They're best said aloud, in front of a mirror, but you can think or say them to yourself anytime, anywhere!

Once your body starts to feel calmer, it's useful to have an affirmation that works well to soothe your anxious thoughts. The more you repeat a certain mantra, the more powerful it will be against anxiety. This is because each time you think something, the brain believes it that bit more. So, replacing anxious thoughts with positive affirmations weakens your negative beliefs, while strengthening the new, positive ones. Try incorporating an affirmation or two into your morning routine.

Again, what works for you will be unique to you. Here are some ideas for anxiety-soothing affirmations. You can use any of these as they are, adapt them or make up your own on the next page:

- I'm safe.
- I am loved.
- The world is a kind place.
- As I relax, anxiety flows out of me.
- I am capable of anything.
- I can do this.
- One step at a time.
- I can do the next right thing.
- I am brave.
- I am in control.
- I can let go of what I cannot control.
- This will pass.
- It's OK to make mistakes.
- I trust myself.
- I have everything I need.
- I can cope.
- I trust the process.

**Write your own ideas
for affirmations here:**

FACTS VS OPINIONS

Anxiety has an annoying habit of making opinions seem like facts, for example:

Fact: I got held up at work and couldn't help my daughter with her homework.

Opinion: I'm failing as a parent. Now she's going to fail at school because of me.

Anxiety takes a fact and twists it into a thinking error. It's hard for our minds to just leave a fact alone and not make an opinion out of it. So instead, try to find the lesson, like this:

Fact: I got held up at work and couldn't help my daughter with her homework.

Opinion: I feel guilty that I wasn't there for my daughter, but she managed fine because I've taught her to be independent. I've learned that I should get better at saying "no" when I'm asked to work late and show more trust in my daughter to cope by herself.

See how the fact doesn't change, but the opinion is much more positive?

Can you think of a fact that brings you anxiety?

Fact:

Now think about an anxious opinion that your mind has invented from this fact...

Opinion:

Can you think of an alternative opinion? It might be positive, like: "I'll do really well..." or neutral, such as: "I can't know how it will turn out" – whichever works for you.

REFRAMING THOUGHTS

Anxiety feeds off negative self-talk which has been shaped by past experiences and unhelpful assumptions we have about ourselves, others and the world we live in. Here are some common examples of negative thinking:

- **You will be unsuccessful: "It's pointless even trying; I know I can't do that."**
- **You will be unable to cope: "I won't know what to say if my manager asks me a question. I will go bright red."**
- **Bad things will happen: "What if I get lost?" "Everyone will laugh at me." "People will think I'm weird."**
- **You will get things wrong: "I never get anything right."**
- **Other people are negatively judging you: "People think I look stupid/ugly/odd/unprofessional etc."**

Thoughts and responses like these are unhelpful:

- **They make you feel unpleasant and increase your anxiety.**
- **They are demotivating and don't encourage you to try things or challenge yourself to do something new and different.**
- **They stop you from living your life and enjoying it.**

To help overcome your anxiety, you need to develop more balanced ways of thinking. One of the best ways to silence the negative chatter is to "reframe" your thoughts. It's a powerful technique used by therapists and psychologists and, just like we explored in the previous exercise, there is always a calmer or more positive way of looking at any situation.

Here are some more useful things to ask yourself to help reframe anxious thoughts:

What advice would I give my best friend in this situation?

What would someone with high self-esteem do in this situation?

What advice would a wise, calm and peaceful person give to me?

Can I try a different method or strategy?

What can I learn from this?

Can I make this thought ten per cent kinder to myself?

What if this thought is just a thought and I don't need to do anything about it?

What would a positive outcome look like?

What would a neutral outcome look like?

USING MINDFULNESS TO BEAT ANXIETY

When you're feeling anxious, you're often overly concerned with what might happen in the future. Mindfulness can be a useful way to connect you with the present. It focuses your mind on what is going on right now and reminds you that you can manage this moment without being overly reactive or overwhelmed by what's going on around you.

Here's a mindful exercise for when you need to distract yourself from anxiety.

Mindful feet

Sit or stand – whichever is more comfortable, as long as your feet are touching the ground. Think about the soles of your feet. You don't need to look at them: just bring your mind's attention to them.
What can the soles of your feet feel? What sensations, temperatures and textures are you aware of?

Think about the tips of your toes, and then slowly move your attention along the bottom of your feet until you get to your heel.

Thinking hard about the soles of your feet means that your mind can't be taken up with anxious thoughts, as it's too busy being in the moment. Once you've mastered this exercise you can try being mindful in other situations, such as...

Taking a mindful walk outside

We've already learned that movement can be helpful in reducing anxiety so if you can do it mindfully it'll be double the benefit! As you walk, turn your attention to the world around you. What do you see, hear, smell and feel? Is the sun warming your face? What does the air feel like against your skin? When anxious thoughts intrude, acknowledge them and then return to being mindful of your activity.

Doing some mindful chores

As you go about the tasks of your day, give your undivided attention to what you are doing, even if it's something you might usually find boring, like cleaning or washing the dishes. Use your senses to immerse yourself in the present moment. Inhale the clean scent of the soap or feel the temperature of the warm water and tickling sensation of the bubbles in the washing-up bowl. When you catch your mind wandering, simply return your attention to what you are doing.

Trying progressive muscle relaxation

This technique is helpful for noticing tension or other symptoms of anxiety in your body before the feelings get out of control. You can do this sitting or lying down, or even standing in a long queue. Start at your feet and notice how they feel. Wiggle your toes, roll your ankles and flex your feet to release tension. Notice how it feels to let the muscles of your feet relax. Then, move to your calves, noting how they feel, tensing and releasing them. Gradually progress up your body until you reach the very top of your head, concentrating on each muscle group in turn. If your mind begins to wander, just return your attention to what you are doing.

BREAKING THE WORRY CYCLE

Anxious thoughts can go round and round in your head, leading to other worries and new imagined scenarios, before circling back to the origin of your anxiety. Often these worries are hypothetical – the "what if" type scenarios – and one anxious thought can easily feed into the next, escalating your anxiety even more. With all these different negative thoughts going around inside your head, it's easy to get stuck in a thought spiral, a bit like this:

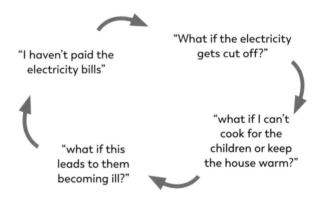

"I haven't paid the electricity bills"

"What if the electricity gets cut off?"

"what if I can't cook for the children or keep the house warm?"

"what if this leads to them becoming ill?"

So how can you break the cycle? Anxious thought spirals are hard to ignore. Often, the answer is to listen to what your anxiety is trying to tell you.

Try writing down all the thoughts that anxiety is bringing into your mind, no matter how unlikely they might seem:

Can you see how your anxiety is trying to keep you safe? Even if it gets a bit (or a lot) carried away sometimes, your brain's number-one job is to protect you from danger. It's like your own in-built early-warning system.

Now ask yourself, can any of these worries be solved with a practical solution? Consider whether it's a worry you can do something about now. Is there a specific plan you can put in place to overcome the worry? For instance, you might be worrying about missing a deadline – can you create a plan to help you achieve it? Or make some extra time in your schedule?

If you know the thought is an unhelpful (and an unlikely) one, you can simply let it go. Try saying out loud, in your head or in writing:

"Thank you, anxiety, I'll keep that in mind, but it's not relevant right now."

Writing down and acknowledging the possibilities that your anxious brain has imagined will make it feel easier to let them go from your mind. Don't forget to wave them goodbye!

JOURNALING

Writing down your anxious thoughts is a brilliant habit to get into. Not only is it a great way to let them out of your mind, but it also helps you to choose different, calmer thoughts and ideas to replace them with.

Writing in a diary or journal before bed each night can help you to fall asleep more easily. Emptying your head of all the things that are bothering you can clear your mind, ready for the important business of sleeping! You don't need anything fancy to get started – any notebook will work (although it is the perfect excuse for some nice new stationery).

You can simply write down your thoughts – or try this everyday bedtime journaling exercise:

Something that's troubling me:

What I would say to myself or do if I wasn't afraid:

Journaling can be helpful. It's also a great idea to talk through any worries or problems you have with someone you trust.

TOP TIPS FOR JOURNALING

- Start by writing for between 5 and 15 minutes but keep going for as long as it takes to unload your worries.

- Review and reflect on what you've written. Do any of your worries have a practical solution? Or can you change how you think about something?

- Try using some of the tips we've already explored in this book to challenge your worries, such as reframing your thoughts and checking whether what you've written is fact or opinion.

If you're struggling to find the right words to start, you could always use one of the following prompts to help you:

List three things you would do if you weren't afraid...

Write down some of the kindest things you can do for yourself if you're having a difficult day...

Jot down one thing you look forward to every day and why...

What does your best day look like?

Write down something you forgive yourself for...

Write down a fear and then rationalize it so it's no longer scary...

List some of the past challenges you've overcome...

Describe how you want to feel today — what do you need to make that happen?

**Use this page to try journaling, using some
of the ideas suggested in this section.**

YOU ARE OK EXACTLY AS YOU ARE

There's a lot in this book about lowering anxiety and having more control over your anxious thoughts, and it might feel like you should be quickly seeing changes or improvements... You might even feel anxious about still feeling anxious!

No matter what, you will always have ups and downs in life. It's OK to go at your own pace – things take as long as they take, and your emotional well-being is not a race or a competition. It's OK to be exactly where you are. It's very, very OK to find this process difficult.

Self-improvement is always a good thing but it's challenging because it asks you to confront aspects of yourself that you probably feel negatively about. This can be uncomfortable and it can be difficult to stay motivated as a result. The key is to maintain a positive focus, which will not only help you better accept yourself, but it'll also make it easier for you to achieve your self-help goals.

If you need a quick shot of positivity, try some of these ideas. There's space for writing more that suit you on the following page:

- **Write down three things you're good at**
- **Write down three things you're grateful for**
- **Go outside and take five big breaths of fresh air, deep into your lungs**
- **Leave a note on a loved one's pillow telling them how much you appreciate them**
- **Make plans for your next day off to give you something to look forward to**
- **Give yourself permission to laugh about something silly**

Learning about your mind and emotions and applying that knowledge to your thoughts and feelings *is* difficult. You can take things one step at a time, and you can also take a step back, retrace your steps or stand still for a while. It gets easier when you take the pressure off.

BUILDING TRUST

Anxiety usually strikes because we fear not being in control. For example, you are likely to feel anxious in social situations because you have no power over what others think about you, and that can seem really threatening. You might try to have some control over it by not really being yourself when you're around others – whether that's by keeping quiet, telling lots of jokes or something else.

The antidote to feeling the need to control everything is to build trust – in other people but also, especially, in yourself.

When you trust yourself, you value your own opinion of yourself more than other people's. You trust that you can ask for help if you need it and you know that you'll cope, even if things don't go quite the way you planned.

The good news is that you're already building up your self-trust. Every time you choose a kind, patient, positive or calm thought over an anxious one, you believe a little more that your mind can be a gentle, supportive place. Every time you take the time to listen to your body and help yourself relax, you trust in your resilience a little more.

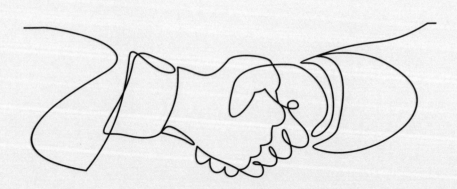

KEEPING A PROMISE TO YOURSELF

A great way to build up self-trust is to make a promise to yourself and keep it for a week. Choose something small and achievable like: "I promise to replace my mid-morning coffee with a healthy smoothie."

Make keeping the promise as easy as possible – for example, make sure you have all the ingredients you need to make a smoothie in the fridge. If you miss a day, don't be hard on yourself – if you feel annoyed, that's a great sign that you're taking it seriously and you're committed to succeeding, which will help to promote an even greater trust in yourself. Just remember to keep the promise the next day instead.

What promise will you make to yourself this week?

Promise tracker

Keep track of your promise to yourself here.

- ☐ **Monday**
- ☐ **Tuesday**
- ☐ **Wednesday**
- ☐ **Thursday**
- ☐ **Friday**
- ☐ **Saturday**
- ☐ **Sunday**

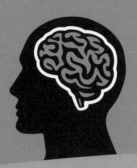

Part 4:
Facing Your Fears

Sometimes it feels like fear is holding us back and stopping us from fulfilling our dreams and living life to its full potential. Perhaps you're afraid of flying and it's stopping you planning a vacation, or perhaps your fear of public speaking is preventing you from making a speech at your brother's wedding. Whether it's a specific activity that makes you afraid, or your fear comes from within — such as fear of failure — the chances are it's not just stopping you from doing the thing you're scared of, it's probably affecting other areas of your life too.

Once you learn to face your fears, you will begin to see that you can cope with anxiety. The things that make us anxious are often not as bad as you imagine — those negative feelings should fade over time, and you'll be back in charge instead of letting anxiety make the decisions for you.

FEELING THE FEAR AND DOING IT ANYWAY

It's in our nature to avoid the things that we know make us anxious, but the way that anxiety can be beaten is by stepping out of your comfort zone and doing things that can seem hard or even anxiety-provoking. When you face your fears, you will see that you can cope with more than you think, and your worries will become easier to deal with.

The truth is you might never feel 100 per cent ready to try the things that make you feel anxious. Bravery isn't the absence of fear – it's doing things while you're still scared.

It may be tricky at times but it can be useful to remember why you want to beat your anxiety as this will motivate you to try.

A big part of facing our fears involves learning to trust ourselves – when we trust that we have the strength of mind and resilience to overcome a challenge, it becomes that bit easier to achieve our goals. Try to reframe how you perceive fear – rather than see it as a negative emotion, see it as an opportunity for you to grow and develop as a person. The reality is, if you keep saying, "When I'm no longer afraid, then I'll do it", you'll be putting it off forever. Fear is part of the package – embrace it.

> I learned that courage was not the absence of fear, but the triumph over it. The brave man is not he who does not feel afraid, but he who conquers that fear.
> Nelson Mandela

STAY IN YOUR STRETCH ZONE

Facing your fears is really important. You can't beat anxiety without acting courageously, but it's also key to not overdo it. Psychologists have developed a theory of three "zones" for anxiety.

- **Your comfort zone is where you feel most calm – anxiety is low and things are predictable.**

- **Your stretch zone is where you're challenging yourself – here is where you can face your fears. You feel anxious and uncomfortable but in control in your stretch zone.**

- **The panic zone is where your body can no longer cope. Anxiety is too high and you feel totally overwhelmed.**

So it's good to go at your own pace. Slipping into the panic zone isn't a disaster but it can set you back and make facing your fears more difficult next time. When you're doing something that makes you feel anxious, take it slow and remember that it's OK to take breaks or try again another day.

TAKE YOUR TIME

It's important that you feel as in control as possible when you're doing the things that scare you, so it's OK to go at your own pace.

A great way of making sure you go at a speed that works for you is to break things down into steps. In CBT this is called an "exposure ladder". The idea is that each step gets you closer to facing your fear and realizing you can do it. When you have small steps between you and something difficult, it makes it a more manageable process.

Start by writing your goal at the top, like in the example. Then break it down into smaller steps – the key, just like a real ladder, is to make the steps small enough to climb easily. If they're too large, it'll be harder for you to reach your goal.

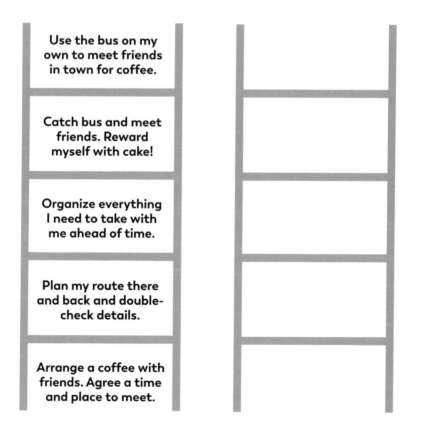

Use the bus on my own to meet friends in town for coffee.

Catch bus and meet friends. Reward myself with cake!

Organize everything I need to take with me ahead of time.

Plan my route there and back and double-check details.

Arrange a coffee with friends. Agree a time and place to meet.

A PLAN FOR WHEN ANXIETY STRIKES

Hopefully, you'll have picked up some useful tips and techniques already from the previous parts of this book. Now it's time to create a plan for when you start to feel anxious.

When you're feeling high anxiety, it can be difficult to think straight, so putting together a written plan when you're calm is a helpful thing to do in preparation. There is no quick fix, or one-size-fits-all option to manage anxiety; what works for one person may not work for the next. It's important to have an anxiety-busting toolbox at your disposal so you can pick a strategy that works for you in your current situation.

Pick and mix from these ideas, and add your own to the next page:

Take a break

Meditate

Sing

Log off

Take three deep breaths

Listen to my calming playlist

Say an affirmation

Go for a run

Do some yoga stretches

Put my hand on my heart

Light some fragranced candles

Write in my journal

Go for a walk

Do some star jumps

Take a bath

Talk to someone

Use my weighted blanket

Have a glass of water

Have a snack

Check in with my five senses

Write your own ideas for your anxiety action plan here.

HOPEFUL JOURNALING

At the start of each day, try visualizing the best possible outcome and write it down in your journal. You can do this every morning, especially when you've got a daunting or anxiety-provoking 24 hours ahead of you.

Not only will this help you focus your thoughts on something positive, but it will also have the added benefit of helping you think of solutions to the things that are worrying you in the day ahead. This is because we often know the answer to our problems deep down and journaling provides a safe and positive place for us to access our subconscious and work out the solution. When we're honest with ourselves about our problems, the answer we're looking for is often staring us in the face!

Think about how you'd like the day to go, what feelings you'd like to experience, what you'd like to achieve and, if you can, how you think you might do it. Be hopeful but realistic – this isn't meant to make you feel inadequate or overburden you. Look at it more like a wish list for the day. For starters, try finishing the prompts below. Try it every morning in your notebook or journal:

Today I will...

I'm going to feel...

I will achieve...

To do this, I will need to...

I will look after myself by...

Remember, journaling helps us open up about the things that matter to us the most. The thoughts, feelings and events you record in your journal might not seem that important when you write them down, but make sure you take the time to review what you've written and use the experience to get a sense of what you enjoy most in life. If you keep coming back to the same idea — for instance, leaving a stressful job and striking out on your own — it's obvious this is important to you, and you can use the idea as a motivator when you're finding things difficult.

LET YOUR FEELINGS OUT

Saying how you feel, particularly if the emotion is negative, is one of the hardest things you can do. It's often much easier to offer up a standard "OK, thanks", response when someone asks how we are – even if we're crying inside. We've all done it, and no doubt we'll do it again at some point. There's no shame in this – letting our feelings out sometimes feels like we're uncorking a bottle full of negative thoughts. We worry that once the cork's gone, all those bad feelings will come tumbling out and we won't be able to control them.

The problem is, for us to process how we feel and move towards a less anxious state, we need to be able to express ourselves. When feelings get stuck inside us, they've got nowhere to go, which means they build up to a point where we end up feeling worse.

When you're anxious, you don't need to pretend that it's not hard. It can be good to practise some phrases to use when you're feeling worried, whether you're facing your fears or you're in a situation that's making you feel panic. That way you can concentrate on calming your body, rather than coming up with things to say.

On the next page you'll find some ideas for how to express yourself when your anxiety levels feel high. There's also some space to add your own.

Something about this is making me uncomfortable

I need to take a break

It's been a difficult day

I'm struggling a bit today; I just need a bit of space

This is really hard

I need some reassurance

To be honest, I'm feeling a bit nervous/unhappy/ stressed/worried

I'm feeling so anxious

I need to leave now – I'll catch up with you later

I need some quiet time – talk later?

Can you help me break this down?

Handling our emotions is never easy, but learning to express them with confidence is one of the most important things we can do for our mental well-being.

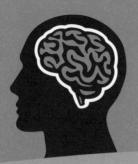

Part 5:
Looking After Your Body and Mind

When life gets busy it's easy to forget to check in with ourselves. Whether we're hard-working parents, or in a demanding job — or sometimes both — we can feel like we're constantly juggling a bucket-load of responsibilities, coming at us from all directions, with no respite or end in sight. Little wonder our own needs get pushed to the bottom of the never-ending to-do list, and before we know it, we're running on empty. Often, we don't realize our well-being is suffering until we reach crisis point and our carefully constructed anxiety-proof barriers come crashing down around us.

Self-care isn't selfish — it's medicine for your mind and body. It's as vital as any other anxiety therapy you might be considering. Read on to find out how to take good care of yourself and minimize anxiety at the same time.

SELF-CARE AND ANXIETY

While anxiety is a normal, healthy emotion, research shows that the more you look after your body and mind, the more resilient you are and the faster you can bounce back from anxious moments.

Developing a well-rounded approach to self-care can help to lessen how often our anxious thoughts intrude on our daily lives. Think about it – you're so much better equipped to manage what life throws at you after a good night's sleep, a healthy meal and a good helping of downtime. And sometimes, it's as simple as that!

Self-care is anything you do for yourself that makes you feel better – whether that's grabbing half an hour to listen to classical music or treating yourself to a fresh haircut or going for a run. If it improves the way you feel in your mind and body, then you're on the right track. It's all about making a deliberate and conscious choice to put yourself first. This may not feel comfortable or OK for all of us, particularly if one of your roles involves caring for young children or other family members but know this: the better you feel, the better you will be in all areas of your life – from work to family to friendships. And what's good for your well-being is without doubt good for anxiety too. In fact, any activity that makes you feel more relaxed can help to reduce symptoms of stress and lift your mood.

The good news is self-care doesn't have to involve a huge time commitment and it doesn't have to cost much either. In fact, many self-care activities are free. You might just relax with a good book, take a walk outside or have a scented bubble bath. It's about making a commitment to putting yourself first and sticking to it – even if it's just for a short time every day.

You might already know what self-care works best for you – if so, just keep doing it – but if you need fresh ideas or a different approach there are plenty of ideas on the following pages. For starters, you could try one of these:

- **Drink lots of water – it sounds simple, but water is just as important for brain health as it is for our bodies.**
- **Go for a brisk walk – better still, borrow a dog for added benefit!**
- **Take a relaxing bath with your favourite essential oil.**
- **Say no to something you don't want to do and don't feel guilty about it either!**
- **Crank up your favourite music and have a dance.**
- **Watch your favourite film under a blanket.**
- **Try a new healthy recipe.**
- **Make a list of five or more things you like about yourself.**
- **Spend time with the people you care about most in the world, whether they're human or animal!**

BEING MINDFUL OF SOCIAL MEDIA

Social media is a brilliant tool for connecting and keeping in touch with others, finding out about the world, shopping and expressing yourself. There are a lot of good things to be said for social media, but at the same time it can increase anxiety and have a negative effect on your mental health.

Have you ever felt anxious about social media? Perhaps you worry about how you come across or compare yourself to others online. Maybe you've been a victim of someone else's vitriol or you've been trolled.

Next time you use social media, take a moment to pay attention to your mind and body. What thoughts are coming up for you? What sensations can you feel in your body? Just a few words for each is fine, then mark on the scale how anxious you feel.

Before going on social media, I feel...

Anxiety level: /10

While I'm on social media, I feel...

Anxiety level: /10

After using social media, I feel...

Anxiety level: /10

FIND YOUR CREATIVITY

Creativity is your mind's way of playing, and there's no right or wrong way to be creative. This means it's an incredibly powerful way to calm anxiety because you don't need to worry about the outcome. When we can enjoy creating in this way it's called "state of flow" – you're in the moment, letting your mind work its magic and having fun.

Creating something is also great for our self-esteem and sense of achievement; it's unique and personal to us, and it's brilliant for exercising our imaginations. It also teaches us to trust in our own emotional intelligence, meaning we'll be better at finding solutions to life's challenges.

Of course, it doesn't always feel so easy. When you sit down to write the next bestseller and you realize your five-year-old has better story ideas than you, that doesn't feel quite so good! The best anti-anxiety creative activities are ones where you don't place expectations on yourself. You could try:

Colouring

Research has shown that colouring-in significantly helps people with anxiety to stay calm. It works just like meditation, making it easier for them to relax and be at peace. There's a reason adult colouring books are some of the most popular on the market!

Creative writing

Poetry, memoir, short stories, opinion pieces – there are so many options for unleashing your inner writer. If you're digitally-minded, you could even start your own blog.

Drawing

Drawing is a great activity for mindfulness – all you need is a pencil and some paper!

BE KIND TO YOURSELF

Studies have found that the voice you use to speak to yourself is one of the biggest influences on your mental well-being. Those who have a kind and patient inner voice can comfort themselves in times of worry, stress or sadness. However, many of us have an internal voice that criticizes us and attacks our self-worth. Sometimes this voice may have originated from a parent or overly critical adult when you were growing up, or perhaps it is a result of your present life experiences. You may not even know when your negative inner voice began, but it's important to know that you don't have to listen to it anymore.

If your inner voice is less like a best friend and more like a bully, you'll find it harder to ignore the negative emotions that feed your anxiety. A critical inner voice is likely to say comments such as:

- **You can't cope**
- **You're weak**
- **You're a failure**

- **You're not a good person**
- **You're useless**

The good news is you can make your inner voice kinder. It takes dedication, but you can do it. The first step is to recognize when your inner voice is talking.

Think back to a time you felt anxious or overwhelmed. How do you feel about that past version of yourself when you felt so anxious? Write it down here:

The things you've written should give you a good idea of your inner voice: yours is a positive one if you've voiced kind words. However, if your inner voice is unkind and makes you feel ashamed for having struggled in the past, you could do with showing yourself a little more compassion.

What could you say to the anxious, past version of yourself that would be more supportive? Imagine what someone who loves and cares about you might say. An example of a nurturing, compassionate statement might be:

- **I'm really proud of your achievements.**
- **You deserve to feel proud of yourself; you earned it.**
- **You're so talented.**
- **You're the bravest person I know.**

Now write what you would say to yourself to be more supportive:

GROW YOUR SELF-LOVE

Self-care is an essential part of self-love. Taking time out to do something for ourselves that makes us feel better, is the ultimate act of self-love – you can't have one without the other! But self-love is a little deeper than that. It's about understanding yourself in a way that perhaps no one else does and having a deep and meaningful appreciation of yourself. If we're able to connect with ourselves in this way and accept who we are – warts and all – we have a much better chance of showing ourselves compassion, especially when we're anxious, which is when we need self-love the most.

Learning to love and trust your mind and body is the greatest gift you can give yourself, as well as one of the strongest ways to fight anxiety. Try this self-love gratitude exercise for a quick and easy reminder to yourself of why you're amazing.

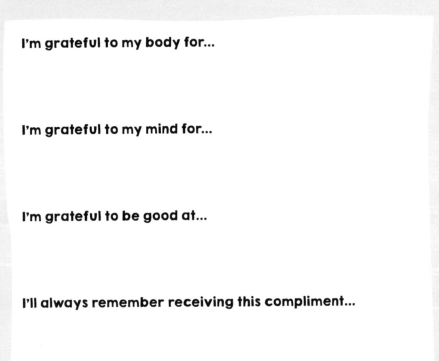

I'm grateful to my body for...

I'm grateful to my mind for...

I'm grateful to be good at...

I'll always remember receiving this compliment...

CULTIVATING SELF-LOVE

- Don't fall into the comparison trap. It's all too easy in the age of social media to compare our own lives with other people's, covet what they have and then feel disappointed with our own lives as a result. Don't forget, most people only share their "highlights" on social media, giving us a very unrealistic portrayal of the normal ups and downs of everyday life.

- Set yourself healthy boundaries. Be able to say "no" to the things that are negatively impacting on your life – such as work overload, unhealthy relationships and non-essential commitments. Cutting the things that harm your well-being out of your life is one of the kindest things you can do for yourself.

- Forgive yourself and let past shame go. Learn to grow from your mistakes rather than use them as a stick to beat yourself with. When the people we love make a mistake, we forgive them – we should apply the same rule to ourselves.

- Make friends with yourself. Show yourself the same love and respect that you'd extend to your loved ones. Allow yourself time for self-exploration and self-reflection.

HEALTHY BODY, HAPPY BRAIN

All kinds of physical exercise help to reduce anxiety, from walking to team sports, and dance classes to boxing.

Movement contributes to freeing our minds from anxious thoughts by bringing our focus into our bodies. When we move, we release tension and calm our emotions. It doesn't have to involve running a marathon or going to the gym five times a week – although, if those things help then by all means do! It's more important to just *move*, whether that's going for a stroll around the park, weeding the plant pots or doing some chair-based exercises.

It makes sense to build exercise and movement into your daily routine as part of your anxiety-busting toolbox. Even if you only manage 10 minutes a day, it will help to regulate your emotions and calm anxiety.

Activities to try at home:

- There are lots of yoga and exercise videos available online for beginners all the way up to more advanced cardio workouts – for most, you just need a soft surface or yoga mat, and bottles of water can double up for weights.

- Do some household chores. Scrubbing, vacuuming, tidying, gardening, DIY – all involve movement, so they all count!

- If you have mobility issues or find it difficult to stand and/or move about, there are lots of chair-based exercises available online.

- Even simple things such as running up and down the stairs or doing some seated bounces on a yoga ball in front of the TV will help to get your heart rate up.

Activities to try outside the home:

- **Walk more than usual – take the longer route home or park further away from the school or office. If you're at work, don't fall into the trap of having lunch at your desk – go and stretch your legs, even if it means just walking to the end of the road and back.**

- **Grab some friends and the dog and play a game of frisbee or football in the local park – you're never too old for playtime!**

- **See what the local sports centre has to offer – there's normally a class to suit everyone, whether you're a fan of Zumba, table tennis or tai chi, it will also enable you to meet new people too.**

- **The health benefits of swimming are well known and the act of being in the water and feeling weightless also helps to calm your mind and body.**

- **Running or rambling in a natural environment helps us feel rooted and connected to the world around us and can provide a calming environment away from the things that cause us anxiety.**

And when it's all a bit too much...

Just do what you can when you can. You're only accountable to yourself – no one else. It's completely normal to have days when you wake up excited to get out there, and other days when just looking at your trainers fills you with dread. And that's OK – just be adaptable and kind to yourself. Have a break and try again when you're feeling better.

EXERCISE TRACKER

Have a think about your daily and weekly schedule – jot it down here and see where you can fit some exercise in each day:

Monday	
Tuesday	
Wednesday	
Thursday	
Friday	
Saturday	
Sunday	

Once you've worked out when you're going to fit your exercise in, you can use a chart like the one below to record each activity as you do it. After a week, you can look back and see how hard you've worked, which will motivate you to keep going! Don't forget to tick off every glass of water and include a goal for the week, such as walk 10,000 steps a day or go swimming three times, to give you something to work towards.

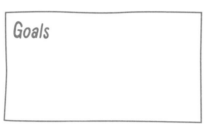

Goals

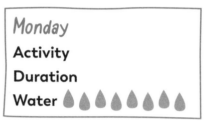

Monday

Activity

Duration

Water

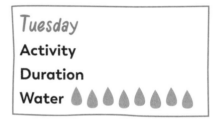

Tuesday

Activity

Duration

Water

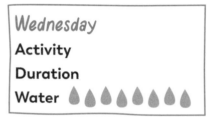

Wednesday

Activity

Duration

Water

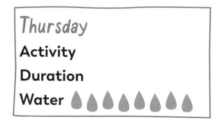

Thursday

Activity

Duration

Water

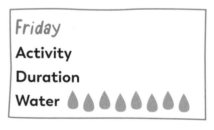

Friday

Activity

Duration

Water

Saturday

Activity

Duration

Water

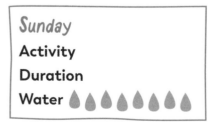

Sunday

Activity

Duration

Water

EAT WELL

Ever felt hangry? How about hanxious? It's a thing! When you go too long without food, your blood glucose levels drop and your body releases hormones to keep you going. These hormones have a powerful effect on your emotions, meaning you're more susceptible to becoming angry, upset or anxious.

So next time you feel anxiety building up, ask yourself – are you hungry or thirsty? If so, grab a healthy snack or drink and you'll notice your anxiety become a little more manageable.

Best anti-anxiety snacks

Look for snacks that are high in vitamins and release energy slowly – these will help you to avoid hanxiety-inducing blood-glucose crashes.

- Probiotic yoghurt
- Berries
- Almonds

- Guacamole
- Wholewheat crackers
- Toast with peanut butter and sliced banana

Top tip

It sounds simple but avoiding foods that are difficult to digest, such as fried or processed foods, is also helpful for managing anxiety. They won't cause anxiety but the stress they put on your body during digestion can increase distress. And who wants to cope with indigestion on top of an anxiety attack?

SLEEP WELL

The better you sleep, the more in control of your emotions you'll be while you're awake. But this can be hard to achieve if anxiety makes it hard for you to get some rest.

A good night-time routine is the best way to ensure that getting to sleep becomes as straightforward as possible. Turn off all screens at least an hour before you plan to go to bed – the blue-tinged light can disrupt your circadian rhythm – and do something enjoyable and relaxing like taking a bath, writing in a journal or reading a chapter of a book. It's less about the activity and more about getting used to doing the same relaxing things each night – forming a habit means that your body will notice the signals that it's time to wind down each evening.

What's your night-time routine?

Try recording your sleeping habits on the tracker on the following pages for the next week. Look for any emerging patterns. For instance, did you sleep better on the days you got some fresh air and/ or exercise? Was your sleep affected on the days you had a glass of wine in the evening? Keeping a sleep diary in this way can help us to see any adjustments we may need to make to our lifestyles to ensure we give ourselves the best possible chance of some shut-eye.

Complete in the morning						
Today's Date						
Time I went to bed last night						
Time I woke up this morning						
How long I took to fall asleep last night						
Total amount of sleep last night						
How awake did I feel when I got up this morning? 1 - Wide awake 2 - Awake but a little tired 3 - Sleepy						

Number of caffeinated drinks and time when I had them today	Number of alcoholic drinks and time when I had them today	Amount of time spent outside today	Exercise times and lengths today	How sleepy did I feel during the day today? 1 - So sleepy I struggled to stay awake during much of the day 2 - Somewhat tired 3 - Fairly alert 4 - Wide awake
Complete in the evening				

BEDTIME YOGA

It's official — anxiety is a sleep thief.

We know that a good night's sleep helps us to face the day ahead and gives us the best possible chance of managing our anxiety, but when sleep is elusive — which it often is when your mind is plagued by worries — it feels like we spend our days dragging our heels and walking through a thick fog.

While it's unrealistic to expect to get into bed every night with a completely empty head — although we can but dream — there are certain things we can do to give ourselves the best possible start to our sleep journey. One of those things is ensuring we're totally relaxed before our head hits the pillow.

If you need a bedtime relaxation routine, try the simple yoga stretches on the next page to get you in the best possible headspace for some serious slumbering.

If you haven't tried these yoga poses before, please refer to a yoga book or online resource.

Hero pose

Child's pose

Upward dog

Camel pose

Butterfly fold

Bridge

Knee-to-chest

Corpse pose

BEDTIME BODY SCAN

If you find yourself getting anxious when you're trying to get to sleep, you're not alone. Many people struggle with this, and there's no one-size-fits-all solution. Try this mindful body scan as part of your night-time routine to help you relax and rest.

Lie in bed and close your eyes. Breathe freely. Begin by thinking about the top of your head. Move slowly down, one body part at a time, checking whether any of them are feeling tense and relaxing those that are. Imagine your body softening into the warmth of your bed. Keep going, slowly, until you reach your toes and relax all of them, one by one.

You might start to feel bored while doing a body scan... that just means it's working! You can't fall asleep while your mind is spinning or concentrating on something entertaining, so let yourself feel bored.

MEDITATION

Research shows that consistently practising meditation can help to reprogramme the neural pathways in our brain and therefore improve our ability to self-regulate our emotions. It can also lower our heart rate and blood pressure, which can have a positive impact on our overall health.

Meditation allows us to change the narrative in our heads and switch our thinking. By familiarizing ourselves with our anxious thoughts, we learn to sit with and accept them – and then let them go. This enables us to see that our thoughts do not define us.

It's all about changing our state of mind and creating a safe space in our heads to retreat to when anxiety strikes.

Try this beginner's exercise for a few days:

1 Find a quiet, comfortable place.

2 Decide how long you'd like to spend meditating but be consistent – even a few minutes every day will be beneficial.

3 Set aside any mental chatter or busy thinking. Take a breath. Tune into the feeling of being present. Check in with your body as you breathe.

4 Acknowledge any physical tensions and mental concerns with kindness and invite them to relax and let go.

5 Tune into your breathing. Feel the breath in your lungs and centre your awareness on the rise and fall of your chest.

6 When you notice that your mind has wandered, bring it back to your breath.

7 End by stretching your body and enjoy a moment of gratitude for life and everything in it.

STAY HYDRATED

Just like those times when you don't get enough sleep or food, not having enough water in your body can make your anxiety worse. A dry mouth, racing heart and feeling too hot can be caused by dehydration or anxiety – their signs are very similar.

It won't solve any real-life problems but having a glass of fresh water will help to calm your anxiety and make you feel that little bit more in control when you're having a tough time. Better still, getting in the habit of having a drinks bottle with you all the time, and sipping from it regularly, will mean that you're always hydrated.

Aim for two litres (three and half pints) of water a day – that's approximately eight tall glasses.

GET INTO NATURE

Being outside has been proven to lower anxiety. Even if it's raining, the combination of fresh air, gentle exercise and natural light will have an instant effect on your mood.

Try to get outside every day. Green spaces such as a local park, forest, beach or riverbank are perfect for exploring. If you can't go too far, you could flex your green fingers and try gardening. You don't even need a garden to grow flowers – just a windowsill, pots, compost and some seeds – and a little nurturing of course! Growing food can also be immensely satisfying, and ensures you'll have a constant stock of healthy fruit and vegetables on your dinner plate.

Other outdoor activities you might like to try to help ease anxiety and boost your mood are:

- **Beachcombing if you're near the sea**
- **Enjoying a picnic in your favourite place**
- **Stargazing**
- **Rambling or hiking in a group**

If getting outside feels too daunting some days, don't forget you can bring nature into your home too:

- **Collect some natural materials and create an artwork or use them to decorate your living space.**
- **Create a cosy nook by the window where you can watch wildlife – even if you're in an urban area you'll be surprised by just how much you can see from a window.**
- **Find a comfortable spot and listen to nature sounds on a digital device – use it as a soundtrack to visualize an outdoor adventure.**

SOOTHING SELF-CARE

Beyond taking care of your basic needs, self-care can also be about soothing yourself when you're feeling anxious.

Using your senses to bring yourself comfort will help to calm your body and slow racing thoughts. Here are some ideas for soothing self-care:

Sight

Watch a feel-good TV show, read a book, watch the world go by

Smell

Have a bath with a scented bath bomb, light an aromatherapy candle, do some baking

Touch

Wrap yourself in a soft blanket, hug someone you love or stroke a pet, play with a stress ball

Sound

Listen to soothing music, sing to yourself, follow a guided meditation

Taste

Eat mindfully, drink hot chocolate

BUILDING A SELF-CARE KIT

A self-care kit is exactly that – a box or collection of things that will help you feel less anxious, more calm and ready to face the world again.

The idea is to provide yourself with everything you need to get back to a level setting again, without having to worry about what to do or where to find the things that you know will help. It removes a level of anxiety from your already anxious state – which can only be a good thing. It doesn't even have to be in a box. You could use a drawer in your dresser, or a shelf in your kitchen cupboard.

Everyone is different, and what helps one person might not help the next, but if you're stuck for ideas, you could include...

- **Scented tissues or a soft handkerchief**
- **Weighted or heated blanket**
- **Aromatherapy neck pillow**
- **Hot-water bottle**
- **Incense or aromatherapy candles**
- **A journal or notepad for recording any anxious thoughts**
- **Daily affirmations or a book of positive quotes**
- **Adult colouring book**
- **Your favourite book**

**What helps you feel balanced again?
Jot some ideas down here:**

Part 6:

Dealing with Whatever Life Throws at You

Life is full of changes — fact. Some of these are planned, such as getting married, moving house or retiring from your job, for example. But we'll also face our fair share of unplanned changes such as losing loved ones unexpectedly, a breakdown in a close relationship, redundancy or unanticipated financial problems. Unexpected things will happen, and you'll face challenges that'll make you feel anxious. But if you're armed with the tools to manage the curveballs as and when they get thrown in your direction, you'll have a better chance of deflecting them before they cause lasting damage to your emotional well-being.

Planning ahead and making sure you have tried-and-tested techniques for calming yourself will help you to feel more in control and capable, whatever happens. And you might just learn something about yourself along the way.

ANXIETY HACKS

When you've got something coming up, like a job interview, that's making you anxious but you need to be ready for, try these anxiety hacks. Let's face it – there's not many among us who can say they enjoy job interviews. If you struggle with social anxiety then meeting strangers in a position of authority, being in an unfamiliar environment, and being judged and evaluated in a formal setting are all likely to be triggers for your anxiety. Exams, presentations, a formal meeting with your boss, going to the dentist or a medical appointment, joining a new club or class, organizing your finances and remembering to pay bills; even going to a busy supermarket or shopping centre – these are just more examples of situations that have the potential to cause unpleasant emotions.

Don't panic; help is at hand! Try some of these hacks next time you've got a challenge to overcome:

Do the hard stuff first

Don't put off the tricky stuff: do it in small chunks alongside something easier. Try setting a timer for 20 minutes – do the dreaded task until time's up, then take a break. For instance, if you're filling in an application form for a college course or a new job and the pressure of writing a good personal statement is making you worried, try drafting some ideas in rough first while filling in some of the easier sections. Take it a paragraph at a time, and stop for a bit in between. Breaking the hard stuff down into bite-size bits makes it less daunting.

Practice makes perfect

Rope in a friend or family member for role-playing duty and practise what you want to say or do with them, as a "dry run". This could also be the perfect forum to speak about any worries you have with your trusted person.

Poor preparation leads to poor performance!

Leaving preparation for any task until the last minute is a recipe for stress and anxiety. Break your tasks down well in advance so you can do a little bit every day and not feel quite so overwhelmed.

The shake down

When you get stuck in your head – finding yourself procrastinating or caught up with anxious thoughts – it helps to literally shake yourself out of it. Stand up, sweep your arms up and down, run on the spot, shake your hips, and get all that nervous energy out of your body. Now you're ready to begin.

Reward yourself

Plan something you can look forward to and schedule it in for after you've completed your challenge. When you're finding things tough and are wondering whether it's worth the stress, focusing on something positive can give you the boost you need to see the challenge through to completion.

On the day of your challenge...

Visualize your success

Take a few moments before you face your challenge, find a quiet spot and close your eyes. Visualize yourself succeeding and what emotions that makes you feel. Channel that energy and use it as a motivator.

And don't forget to breathe!

TALK ABOUT IT

Being anxious might feel embarrassing and be something you think should be concealed. In reality, it's OK to find things difficult, and talking about it helps to lessen anxiety.

Research shows that discussing our feelings can have an instant, positive effect on our emotions – making anxiety, pain, sadness and anger less intense. This could be because naming our emotions activates the right side of the brain (which is responsible for emotional intelligence), so the effect of the amygdala on our thoughts and feelings is reduced.

Talk to someone you're close to and trust – it might feel like your anxiety is obvious to others, but often people can't see it unless you tell them. Most importantly, be gentle with yourself and know that there are people who want to help.

- **If talking face-to-face feels too much, try writing a letter, email or text instead.**

- **There are lots of people you can reach out to: family, trusted friends and work colleagues. You can also talk to your doctor or a therapist about anxiety.**

- **Sometimes talking to other anxiety-sufferers in an online community can help. The benefit of this is that you'll be able to share with a group of people who can empathize with your experiences. You may even be able to help others in return.**

- **When you speak to someone, tell them whether you would like them just to listen or if you are looking for advice.**

- **See the resources list on page 155 for more ideas of where to find support.**

VISUALIZATION

Visualization is a great asset to your self-care toolkit because it can help you to self-regulate your emotions.

Visualization is a form of meditation that involves taking our minds to a different place or state of mind that is completely removed from the situation that is causing us to be anxious. Doing this helps us to minimize the impact of our anxiety and control its effect on us.

Being able to direct our thoughts away from negative thinking is especially useful if you're someone whose anxiety manifests in worry about the future. If we can learn how to steer our minds away from the negative visualization involved in imagining what disasters and challenges life has in store for us, we can learn to look towards a positive future instead.

Visualize this thing you want.
See it, feel it, believe in it.
Make your mental
blueprint and begin.
Robert Collier

If you want to try visualization but don't know how to begin, this exercise is a good starting point:

- **Find a time and place where you're unlikely to be distracted. Make yourself comfortable but alert.**

- **To calm and quieten your mind, start with a breathing exercise. Close your eyes and start to slowly breathe in through your nose and out through your mouth. As you inhale, imagine your abdomen filling with air, like a balloon. As you exhale, let the air escape the balloon slowly, in its own time. This will help you to breathe deeply from your diaphragm, rather than taking the shallow breaths we sometimes do when we're anxious.**

- **Focus on your breathing and let the rhythm of the inhale and exhale calm you.**

- **Next, visualize a safe and relaxing space. This could be anywhere you feel comfortable but try to visualize it from memory. Where is your safe place? Where do you feel secure enough to let go of your worries?**

- **Try to immerse yourself in the whole sensory experience of your safe place. What do you feel? What do you see? What do you smell? Who is there? Can you reach out and touch them?**

- **When you're ready to leave your safe place check in with how you are feeling in real life. Has anything changed?**

Try 5 minutes of visualization to begin with and slowly increase the amount of time that you immerse yourself in your safe space.

If you've got a challenging situation coming up, you can also use visualization to imagine it going well. Scientists have found that imagining doing something stimulates the same parts of your brain as actually doing it. So, when you picture things going well, it's like practice for your brain – you'll subconsciously start to expect a good outcome.

Athletes use visualization to help them run races in their goal times. They picture themselves achieving their aim and this has been proven to make it more likely to happen.

Next time you're feeling anxious about something, use your visualization exercise to imagine it going well.

BREAKING IT DOWN

Some things can feel huge and overwhelming to think about, like that difficult report your boss has asked you to write. Or ending an unhealthy relationship and moving on. Sometimes it feels easier to put it off for another day and hide under the covers. This is called procrastination and it's a common sign of anxiety.

The hardest part about procrastination is that the longer you put off beginning something, the bigger a problem it becomes, especially in the case of something like a business report or presentation, where there's a deadline. Knowing this doesn't usually make it any easier, though!

If you catch yourself procrastinating because of anxiety, don't be too hard on yourself. One great way of beating this cycle is to break tasks down into smaller pieces. You could use the ladder exercise on page 76 to help you. That way, you're faced with several manageable jobs to complete one at a time, rather than a huge mountain of work.

Try using the planner on the next page to help you.

> You don't have to
> see the whole staircase.
> Just take the first step.
>
> Martin Luther King Jr

Weekly goals

- [ ]
- [ ]
- [ ]
- [ ]
- [ ]
- [ ]
- [ ]

Monday

- [ ]
- [ ]
- [ ]
- [ ]
- [ ]
- [ ]

Tuesday

- [ ]
- [ ]
- [ ]
- [ ]
- [ ]
- [ ]
- [ ]

Wednesday

- [ ]
- [ ]
- [ ]
- [ ]
- [ ]
- [ ]
- [ ]

Thursday

- [ ]
- [ ]
- [ ]
- [ ]
- [ ]
- [ ]

Friday

- [ ]
- [ ]
- [ ]
- [ ]
- [ ]
- [ ]
- [ ]

Saturday

- [ ]
- [ ]
- [ ]
- [ ]
- [ ]
- [ ]
- [ ]

Sunday

- [ ]
- [ ]
- [ ]
- [ ]
- [ ]
- [ ]

Weekly goals

- [ ]
- [ ]
- [ ]
- [ ]
- [ ]
- [ ]
- [ ]

Monday

- [ ]
- [ ]
- [ ]
- [ ]
- [ ]
- [ ]
- [ ]

Tuesday

- [ ]
- [ ]
- [ ]
- [ ]
- [ ]
- [ ]
- [ ]

Wednesday

- [ ]
- [ ]
- [ ]
- [ ]
- [ ]
- [ ]
- [ ]

Thursday

- [ ]
- [ ]
- [ ]
- [ ]
- [ ]
- [ ]
- [ ]

Friday

- [ ]
- [ ]
- [ ]
- [ ]
- [ ]
- [ ]
- [ ]

Saturday

- [ ]
- [ ]
- [ ]
- [ ]
- [ ]
- [ ]
- [ ]

Sunday

- [ ]
- [ ]
- [ ]
- [ ]
- [ ]
- [ ]

Weekly goals

- [ ]
- [ ]
- [ ]
- [ ]
- [ ]
- [ ]
- [ ]

Monday

- [ ]
- [ ]
- [ ]
- [ ]
- [ ]
- [ ]
- [ ]

Tuesday

- [ ]
- [ ]
- [ ]
- [ ]
- [ ]
- [ ]
- [ ]

Wednesday

- [ ]
- [ ]
- [ ]
- [ ]
- [ ]
- [ ]
- [ ]

Thursday

- [ ]
- [ ]
- [ ]
- [ ]
- [ ]
- [ ]
- [ ]

Friday

- [ ]
- [ ]
- [ ]
- [ ]
- [ ]
- [ ]
- [ ]

Saturday

- [ ]
- [ ]
- [ ]
- [ ]
- [ ]
- [ ]
- [ ]

Sunday

- [ ]
- [ ]
- [ ]
- [ ]
- [ ]
- [ ]
- [ ]

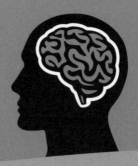

Part 7:
Friendships and Relationships

The relationships we have with other people can be a source of anxiety. When you worry about what others think of you or how they react to you, it can be hard to relax and be yourself. If there's an argument or conflict, it becomes even harder. Navigating personal relationships can be complex at the best of times but when anxiety is also playing a role in how we interact with those around us, it can challenge even the strongest of relationships.

In this chapter we'll explore friendships and relationships with loved ones and look at some strategies for managing anxiety around these interactions.

BEING YOURSELF

It sounds odd but being yourself sometimes feels hard. Often it's easier just to slip into a "role" depending on where you are and who you are with. This is because it's human nature to want to "fit in" and behave how we think others want us to behave – and in a way that portrays us in a good light so that we impress those around us. We might want to cover up aspects of ourselves or our personalities that we're not comfortable with sharing or we're ashamed of. There's nothing wrong with that *per se* but pretending to be anyone other than yourself can be exhausting – and it's also terrible for your mental health.

It's important that we learn to accept ourselves just as we are. That means accepting how we look, having good self-esteem and being happy with where we are in life. When we make friends with ourselves and feel comfortable in our own skins then we can truly be ourselves.

If you want true relationships
in your life – ones that support you
and sustain you through whatever
life throws at you – then you need
to be yourself. If you cannot be yourself,
then people will never really
know the real you.

COMPARING YOURSELF

Comparing yourself to other people is always a bad idea. It's bad for your self-esteem and can leave you feeling anxious that you need to change to measure up. To compound the problem, social media has made it even easier for us to see inside each other's lives, meaning unhealthy comparisons are inevitable.

Comparing your life to other people's also steers your attention away from the positive things in your own life and your achievements. It's important to find a balance between challenging yourself and appreciating yourself as you are.

So how can you stop comparing? The key is to get comfortable with not knowing. As anxiety wants to create a story and know every detail, it will have you making assumptions about other people. For example, you might assume that your colleague has it easy— she leaves work early to fetch her kids from school every day and you still got overlooked for that promotion in favour of her, but the truth could be quite different! What you don't see is that once she's put the kids to bed, she's back at her computer at home working until 11 p.m. each night.

By taking a moment to pause and remind yourself that you don't know anyone else's full story, you give yourself the chance to see the many alternative scenarios that are possible, and this makes it easier to stop comparing yourself.

Try this:
take a deep breath and say,
"I am OK exactly as I am."

BOUNDARY-SETTING BASICS

What are boundaries? They're the limits of what you're OK with. "I don't answer texts after 9 p.m." is an example of a boundary. "I'm free next week, but not before" is another, and so is: "I'm not comfortable with that – it makes me feel really anxious."

Even though boundaries can help to keep us out of uncomfortable situations, communicating them can be a huge source of anxiety. You might worry about hurting someone else's feelings or causing a relationship to break down.

If that sounds like you, it helps to be prepared. For example, if you're going to an event where you know that the host might want you to stay later than you're comfortable with, decide what time you want to leave beforehand. You could even let the host know in advance.

People who care about you will understand and welcome your clarity about your limits and adjust if necessary.

Here are some boundary-setting phrases to get comfortable with:

- No, thank you.
- That's not going to work for me.
- I'd love to stay, but I have to go now.
- That's all I can offer.
- Sorry, I can't.

- I need some space right now, so I'm going to have to pass on that.
- I'm going to say "no" for now. I'll let you know if something changes.
- Please stop doing that. I'm finding it really uncomfortable.

While communicating boundaries clearly is a great skill to master, sometimes it's not practical. You can communicate discomfort by using body language – or simply leave if you ever feel in danger.

TALKING TO FRIENDS AND FAMILY

One of the first steps you can take in your anxiety journey is to acknowledge that you are struggling with anxious thoughts and tell someone close to you – whether that's a family member or a trusted friend. Doing this lets them know that you need support and gives them the opportunity to help you. It also helps to normalize your anxiety so that your friends and family can focus on helping you feel better, rather than it being an awkward subject that no one quite knows how to deal with. It can also help them avoid doing things or creating situations that may trigger your anxiety. For instance, if you tell your loved ones that your panic attacks are triggered by large social gatherings, they won't be upset or take it personally if you don't join them at the next big family party.

If talking to your friends and family about your anxiety makes you anxious, it might help to plan out what you want to say in advance. Use the space below to write down what you'd like to say:

My anxiety is triggered by...

I feel overwhelmed when...

You could help by...

WHAT MAKES A GOOD FRIENDSHIP OR RELATIONSHIP? AND WHAT MAKES A BAD ONE?

Romantically involved or just friends, there are certain qualities that will help you determine whether someone is a good fit for you.

Positive	Negative
Lets you be yourself	Puts you down for who you are
Is fine with you having other friends	Controls who you see
Replies to your messages	Ignores or ghosts you
Is considerate of your feelings	Treats you like your feelings don't matter
Is interested in your thoughts, feelings and experiences	Only talks about themselves
Makes you feel safe	Makes you feel anxious or unsafe
Laughs with you	Laughs at you
You can tell them if they've upset you	Refuses to acknowledge that they've upset you
Accepts "no"	Gets angry or manipulative when told "no"
They want to spend time with you	They will drop you for other plans

WHAT TO DO IF YOU'RE IN A BAD FRIENDSHIP OR RELATIONSHIP

If you're in a friendship or relationship where you feel unsafe or unable to leave, it's not your fault. This can happen to anyone, and the blame lies solely with the person who is treating you disrespectfully. They might use guilt or threats to stop you from leaving, and suffering with anxiety could make this even harder for you to deal with.

Remember: you are entitled to put your comfort and safety first, and you are not responsible for other people's emotions.

There are many people you can talk to if you're unsure about someone in your life or want confidential advice. Think of someone that you know and trust implicitly. Then check out the resources section on page 155. You're not alone and you deserve to be treated with respect.

> **Sometimes you have to forget what you feel and remember what you deserve.**
> Anonymous

MEASURING UP

Being an adult comes with an annoying set of expectations – pressure to do well in your career, finding "the one", getting married, having children, owning your own property, being an amazing parent, looking ten years younger, staying fit and healthy... blah, blah, the list goes on.

But these expectations often don't come from us. Instead, they are foisted on us by society, what we see in the media and sometimes, unfortunately, by those around us. The problem is, when you're under this sort of daily pressure, anxiety about not measuring up to these expectations only serves to make your anxiety worse.

What pressure or expectations do you feel from your family, friends, work, the media or other sources? Write about them here:

On the flipside, sometimes a bit of healthy expectation can motivate you, even if it's irritating – like working until late to achieve that promotion you've got your eye on.

The difference is, the expectation has come out of choice; it's come from your own wants and desires. It can help you to focus and fulfil your potential. In contrast, pressures from outside sources generally aren't helpful and if they're unrealistic, they can make you feel anxious.

Which expectations are helpful to you?

Which expectations are unhelpful to you? What would it be like to let go of them?

Can you use one of the affirmations from this book, or one you've made up yourself, to help you think about one of these expectations differently? For example, if you feel anxious about your body looking different to other people's, you might say to yourself: "I am OK exactly as I am" or "I am more than just my body."

While we can't control other people's expectations, we can influence how we think and feel about them and how much we allow them to bother us.

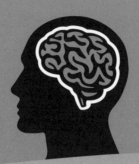

Part 8:
Looking Forward

Anxiety can make the future seem like a dark and negative place, but it doesn't have to be that way. Using the strategies you've learned by reading this book, and your inner strength, you can look forward to a bright and positive future, knowing that you can count on yourself to cope and reach out for help when you need it. In this last section, we'll look at how you can use the things you've learned in this book as part of your everyday life.

A BRIGHTER FUTURE

Working towards a brighter future requires making changes, which can be scary. What we do today affects our tomorrow and that's a big responsibility! Hopefully through reading this book you've been able to see that anxiety doesn't have to stop you from dreaming big and achieving wonderful things. Armed with your anxiety toolkit and a new confidence, you CAN look forward to a brighter future. And just in case you're in any doubt, just remember these key points:

- **The past doesn't define you. It's healthy to acknowledge past mistakes, but once you've done that it's time to move on.**

- **Define your life values and live by them – whether that's "always work hard and do my best" or "show kindness to others". Know what you stand for, but also what you don't, so don't forget to set boundaries too.**

- **Remember to forgive yourself – no one is perfect; despite what they post on social media!**

- **Set goals and work out how you can best achieve them – remember you can always break them down into smaller steps so they're more manageable.**

- **Question and interrogate your decisions – when you set out to achieve something, know why you're doing it. Lead your life with purpose.**

- **And finally, look after yourself – use your self-care kit and try to live a healthy lifestyle.**

GOALS FOR THE FUTURE

Having a goal is a good motivator. Whether you're dreaming big or starting small, you need a strategy to help you achieve it. Your goal might be related to your anxiety, or it could be something you want to accomplish. Use the tracker opposite to write your future goals and how you think you might break them down into manageable steps:

DATE ___ / ___ / ___

GOAL

STEPS

☐

☐

☐

☐

DATE ___ / ___ / ___

GOAL

STEPS

☐

☐

☐

☐

DATE __ / __ / __

GOAL

STEPS

- [ ]
- [ ]
- [ ]
- [ ]

DATE __ / __ / __

GOAL

STEPS

- [ ]
- [ ]
- [ ]
- [ ]

The golden rules of goal setting

- **Think about your priorities and passions – you've got a better chance of achieving your goal if it excites you.**

- **Spend some time researching and thinking about what you need to achieve your goal.**

- **Be prepared to react and respond to changing circumstances – you only have control over your actions, not your circumstances, so your goal may need to adjust along with your situation.**

MY ANXIETY FIRST-AID KIT

If anxiety makes it difficult for you to remember what helps, use this page to write down the things that work for you. If you feel anxiety is getting the better of you, you can refer to this page to help you feel calm again.

I can talk to...

An idea that helps me... (e.g. I can take this one breath at a time)

An activity that helps me... (e.g. visualization)

Remember that... (e.g. I can't control everything)

A movie that makes me feel good...

A song that calms me...

How long since I had a snack or drank a glass of water?

WHAT'S IN THE BOX?

Here's a reminder of some of the ideas we've talked about in this book so you can take back control and manage your anxiety. What's in your toolbox? Write it alongside the other suggestions.

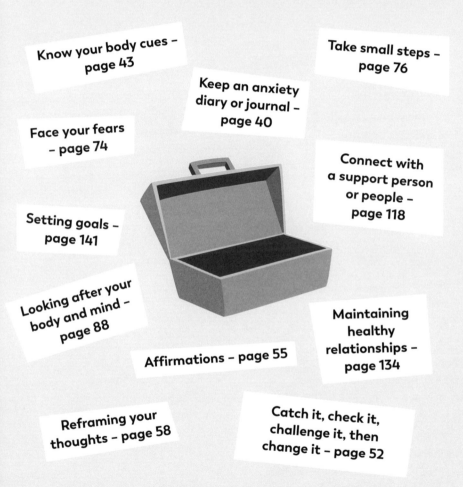

Know your body cues – page 43

Take small steps – page 76

Keep an anxiety diary or journal – page 40

Face your fears – page 74

Connect with a support person or people – page 118

Setting goals – page 141

Looking after your body and mind – page 88

Maintaining healthy relationships – page 134

Affirmations – page 55

Reframing your thoughts – page 58

Catch it, check it, challenge it, then change it – page 52

FIVE WAYS TO WELL-BEING

Research has shown that our long-term well-being can be nurtured if we can incorporate five key actions into our day-to-day lives:

Staying connected

Making time to connect with your loved ones, friends, colleagues and community will contribute to your self-worth and ensure you have a broader support network when times are tough.

Taking notice

Develop an awareness of the here and now and the environment around you. Try to make time in your daily schedule for the mindfulness exercise on page 60.

Keep on learning

Learning something new is a great confidence booster, which is good for our overall well-being. Whether it's trying something new or rediscovering an old interest, taking on a new challenge is a great distraction and it's beneficial for our brain health too.

Being active

As little as 30 minutes every day is all you need to increase your well-being and help relieve anxiety and depression.

Giving

Giving something to another person – whether that's your time, or a friendly listening ear, or a kind word – makes us feel good inside. Voluntary or community work is a brilliant way to get the feel-good factor and you'll be helping others too.

Use the worksheet on the next page to record your own "five ways to well-being".

FIVE WAYS TO
WELL-BEING WORKSHEET

Staying connected	*e.g. having lunch with a friend, cooking a meal for a loved one*
Taking notice	*e.g. 10 minutes of mindfulness before you start your day*
Keep on learning	*e.g. taking up photography, learning how to play tennis*
Being active	*e.g. trying a new woodland trail, walking the kids to school*
Giving	*e.g. paying more compliments to family and friends, volunteering at the local care home*

YOU'RE NOT ALONE

Many of us will struggle with anxious feelings at some point – you're far from alone. Here are a few fellow anxiety sufferers who've been through challenging times and learned ways to conquer anxiety.

When my wife and I split up, I blamed myself completely, even though it was a mutual decision. I tried to be a good husband, but I felt like I'd let everyone down, especially our children. I got into a spiral of negative thinking, and just couldn't move on. I felt like I was on autopilot, but inside I was dying. I thought I'd never get over it. One day I broke down in tears at work and told my colleague everything. He's been an amazing support and encouraged me to speak to my doctor. I'm now seeing a therapist, who has helped me move on. It's hard, but I'm slowly learning to adjust to my new single life.

Andrew, 45

I was signed off work for a year because I was ill. I love my job so I was thrilled when the doctors told me I was well enough to go back, but when I got into the office, I was so anxious I couldn't even speak. Everyone and everything had changed while I was away. I had totally lost my confidence in the work environment. My manager noticed that I was struggling and, together with the HR team and my workplace assistance programme, I was able to feel comfortable at work again.

Priya, 25

When I got really anxious, I used to lash out at others. I said and did some hurtful things to my loved ones that I regret. My friend suggested I start doing some regular exercise to help balance my emotions. I wasn't convinced but I joined a mountain biking club and now I've got an outlet for my emotions. Nothing beats the release of flying down a hill and making it to the bottom in one piece. I don't know what I'd do without it.

Jonny, 32

When my son was diagnosed as being on the autism spectrum, I wasn't sure how we'd cope as a family. I found myself thinking about all the "what-if's" and blamed myself for his condition. I couldn't stop thinking that I hadn't taken care of myself while I was expecting him, and I was somehow to blame. What if I hadn't had that glass of wine? What if I'd eaten better? These were all irrational thoughts, but I couldn't seem to get perspective on it. I was also anxious about his future and how we'd support him. Would people judge him for being "different"? Fortunately, I met a lovely lady whose child also had SEND (Special Educational Needs and Disabilities) and she encouraged me to join a group for parents and children with ASD (Autism Spectrum Disorder). Being among other parents who were experiencing similar challenges to us meant I could voice my anxieties without fear of being judged. It was also great for my son to meet other children and connect with them.

Camilla, 36

SEEKING PROFESSIONAL HELP

If you're struggling with anxiety or any other aspect of mental health, there are lots of organizations out there that can provide help and advice. If you feel like your anxiety is starting to affect your life, you should speak to your doctor or healthcare provider.

Anxiety & Depression Association of America

adaa.org

A not-for-profit organization that aims to improve the quality of life for those with anxiety and other related disorders. Their website includes useful information about anxiety and a "find a therapist" directory.

Anxiety UK

03444 775 774 (helpline)
07537 416 905 (text)
www.anxietyuk.org.uk

Advice and support for people living with anxiety.

Mind (UK)

0300 123 3393
www.mind.org.uk

Includes comprehensive information and support pages, as well as tips for living with anxiety and an online community. There is also a crisis resources page with self-help advice to help you cope.

Campaign Against Living Miserably (CALM) (UK)

0800 58 58 58

www.thecalmzone.net

Provides listening services, information and support, including a webchat, for anyone who needs to talk.

Mental Health America

mhanational.org

Text "MHA" to 741741 to connect with a trained crisis counsellor. Practical advice and support for all aspects of mental health, including links to online communities and tools for long-term wellness.

Samaritans (UK)

116 123

www.samaritans.org

Samaritans provides mental health support and a listening service for those who wish to speak to someone confidentially and without judgement. You can also email Samaritans if you find writing about your anxiety or depression easier, at jo@samaritans.org.

ALTERNATIVE THERAPIES

If you're seeking a more holistic approach to tackling your anxiety, you might like to consider an alternative therapy. Therapies such as acupuncture and herbal supplements have become increasingly popular in recent years, but they often take time to start working so you may have to persevere before you see results. If you're having a panic attack, alternative therapies alone will not be enough, and they often work best if you use them alongside more traditional treatments, such as medication, counselling and CBT. You should always consult your doctor or healthcare provider before trying alternative therapy.

Acupuncture

Acupuncture is an ancient Chinese treatment that involves inserting sharp needles into the upper layers of skin at pressure points of the body that correspond to different organs. The theory goes that by activating natural chemicals in the brain, it can reduce the effects of anxiety. Always find a registered practitioner and speak to your doctor before using acupuncture.

Herbal remedies

Herbal-based supplements are thought to be helpful for mild to moderate anxiety but research in this area is still ongoing. Many herbs can be beneficial for your overall health, which in turn will help your mental health too. You could try:

- **Valerian – its properties are said to be beneficial for sleep.**
- **Vitamin B-12 – is beneficial for the nervous system and can reduce feelings of anxiety.**
- **St John's Wort – research suggests that St John's Wort increases the activity of brain chemicals such as serotonin and noradrenaline which are important mood regulators. It's thought to work best for mild anxiety.**
- **The amino acid L-theanine which is found naturally in green and black tea, is thought to help reduce stress and anxiety.**

You must always check with a doctor before taking herbal remedies, particularly if you're pregnant, breastfeeding or taking other medications, as some can have dangerous side effects.

Aromatherapy

Aromatherapy for anxiety involves using the essential oils found in flowers, leaves, seeds, fruits and roots. When these oils are inhaled or absorbed through the skin, they are thought to be beneficial for anxiety.

They can be added to a bath, a diffuser, inhaled on a handkerchief or as part of a relaxing massage. They must always be used diluted as they come in concentrated form and they can cause allergic reactions, so use with care. You could try:

- **Cedarwood – for anxiety**
- **Camomile – for nervous tension and as a relaxant**
- **Marjoram – for anxiety and insomnia**
- **Sandalwood – for anxiety and depression**

Reflexology

Reflexology involves massaging pressure points on the feet and hands to benefit other parts of the body. A 2017 study found that hand reflexology was particularly beneficial for anxiety. To try it yourself apply pressure to the Heart 7 point (see illustration) just below the crease of your wrist. Massage this area for 1 minute on both hands.

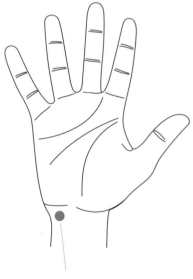

Heart 7

CONCLUSION

Tackling your anxiety will be challenging, but worth it. The important thing is that you've taken the first steps on your journey – congratulations! All you need to do now is keep moving forward. Just take it one step at a time and go at your own pace. It's OK to make mistakes – and it's OK if you find yourself standing still for a bit or even going a few steps back. The path to your goal is always there waiting for you to rejoin it when you're ready, and so is this book – hopefully, you've found some useful ideas and strategies you can use to keep making progress.

Remember that you can cope with whatever life throws at you and that you are never alone – you can reach out for help and people will be there for you. Anxiety is a part of being human but it doesn't have to control your life – you will get there, and you deserve to live your best life. Good luck!

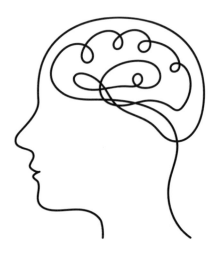

RESOURCES

As well as the organizations detailed on pages 150–151, here are some further sources of inspiration and support that you can refer to during your wellness journey.

Websites

www.nhs.uk/mental-health (UK)

ecouch.com.au (Australia)

www.anxietycanada.com (Canada)

psychcentral.com/anxiety (USA)

Podcasts

Mindset Change (UK)
Anxiety sufferer Paul Sheppard helps you change your mindset to change your life, as he shares the tools, strategies and perspectives to help you boost confidence, motivation, energy and relaxation and feel happier with life.

Mentally Yours (UK)
A weekly mental health podcast with hosts Ellen Scott and Yvette Caster. Listen to interviews and chat with people who have lived with mental illness, from shop workers to celebrities, as well as hosts Ellen and Yvette – who share their own experiences of living with mental health disorders.

Your Anxiety Toolkit (USA)
Kimberley Quinlan discusses OCD, anxiety, panic, depression, eating disorders and CBT in this mindfulness-focused podcast.

Love Your Anxiety (Canada)
Feel inspired and motivated to build a deep and powerful relationship with yourself, with anxiety survivor Emilie Clarke.

The Anxiety Shut-In Hour (Australia)
Hosted by Erin and Anna, who both live with anxiety issues, this podcast tackles the day-to-day experience of anxiety with an approach that is equal parts grounded and light-hearted, with a healthy dose of sarcasm thrown in.

Books

The Anxiety and Phobia Workbook (2020) – Edmund J. Bourne

The Worry Cure: Seven Steps to Stop Worry from Stopping You (2005) – Robert L. Leahy

How to Deal with Anxiety (2015) – Lee Kannis-Dymand and Janet D. Carter

How to Deal with Low Self-Esteem (2015) – Christine Wilding

Negative Self-Talk and How to Change It (2019) – Shad Helmstetter, Ph.D.

Anxiety charities

No Panic (UK) – nopanic.org.uk

Mental Health Foundation (UK) – www.mentalhealth.org.uk

Social Anxiety Association (USA) – socialphobia.org

ReachOut (under 25s, Australia) – au.reachout.com

Online forums, support groups and communities

www.sane.org.uk

support.therapytribe.com/anxiety-support-group (USA)

www.dailystrength.org/group/anxiety (USA)

www.beyondblue.org.au/get-support/online-forums/anxiety (Australia)

www.anxietycanada.com/resources/mindshift-cbt (Canada) – the downloadable MindShift CBT app features access to the online community forum

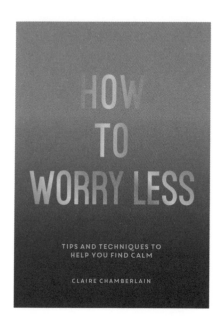

HOW TO WORRY LESS
Tips and Techniques to
Help You Find Calm

Claire Chamberlain

£10.99

ISBN: 978-1-80007-171-1

Paperback

WORRY LESS, LIVE MORE

Worrying is a normal part of the human experience, and it can affect anyone, anywhere, at any stage of life. However, when worry starts to impact our mental and physical well-being, it's time to do something about it.

   In this book you will learn the benefits of mindfulness and meditation, how you can harness the power of positive thinking, and tips and techniques for managing daily stress.

Find out how to:

- Reframe your thoughts and approach stressful situations with greater ease
- Fine-tune your diet to increase your resilience
- Increase your happiness and self-confidence through exercise
- Release stress using relaxation techniques
- Build your own "worry toolkit" of effective coping strategies
- Make sustainable and lasting changes to your habits and behaviours
- Manage your worry in all its guises with this comforting guide for a happier, healthier you.

Ideal for anyone looking to cope with worry, develop stress-management techniques and form positive lifestyle habits.

MY STRESS TRACKER
A Journal to Help You Map Out
and Manage Your Stress Levels

Anna Barnes

£10.99

ISBN: 978-1-78783-533-7

Paperback

KEEP TRACK OF YOU

This tracker is a useful tool to help you document your stress levels over time. Whether you want to understand what makes you feel stressed and why or learn more about your mood patterns, this book is the perfect place to start.

Including a monthly stress tracker, calming activities, relaxation exercises and more, this journal helps you to develop not only an awareness of your stress levels, but also an understanding of how you can manage them.

Have you enjoyed this book?
If so, why not write a review on your favourite website?

If you're interested in finding out more about our books,
find us on Facebook at **Summersdale Publishers**,
on Twitter at **@Summersdale** and on Instagram
at **@summersdalebooks** and get in touch.
We'd love to hear from you!

Thanks very much for buying this Summersdale book.

www.summersdale.com